CAST IRON COOKBOOK

From Stove to Table, Quick & Easy, Everyday Cast Iron Recipes

(Delicious Cast Iron Skillet Recipes You Can Easily Make)

Michele Bronson

Published by Sharon Lohan

© Michele Bronson

All Rights Reserved

Cast Iron Cookbook: From Stove to Table, Quick & Easy, Everyday Cast Iron Recipes (Delicious Cast Iron Skillet Recipes You Can Easily Make)

ISBN 978-1-990334-98-6

All rights reserved. No part of this guide may be reproduced in any form without permission in writing from the publisher except in the case of brief quotations embodied in critical articles or reviews.

Legal & Disclaimer

The information contained in this book is not designed to replace or take the place of any form of medicine or professional medical advice. The information in this book has been provided for educational and entertainment purposes only.

The information contained in this book has been compiled from sources deemed reliable, and it is accurate to the best of the Author's knowledge; however, the Author cannot guarantee its accuracy and validity and cannot be held liable for any errors or omissions. Changes are periodically made to this book. You must consult your doctor or get professional medical advice before using any of the suggested remedies, techniques, or information in this book.

Table of contents

Part 1 1

Introduction 2

Cast Iron Recipes 40

    Cast Iron Chi-Town Deep Dish Skillet Pizza 40

    Cast Iron Thin Crust Caprese Skillet Pizza 43

    Cast Iron Easy Focaccia 46

    Cast Iron New Orleans Pain Perdu 48

    Cast Iron Skillet Fried Chicken Tenders 51

    Southern Skillet Cornbread 54

    Triple Chocolate Brownie Skillet Pie 56

    Cast Iron Buttermilk Brunch Cake 58

Part 2 62

Introduction 63

Chapter 1: Delicious Vegetarian Recipes 64

    Orzo Salad Topped With Buttermilk Dressing 64

    Broccoli- Ham Pasta Salad 65

- Spinach- Chickpea Squash 66
- Vegetarian Bibimbap 68
- Vegetarian Korma 69
- Creamy Barley Salad With Apples 70
- Broccoli Meatballs With Garlic And Tomato Sauce 71
- Tomatillo Pizza-Dillas 73
- Vegetable Meat Loaf 74
- Veggistrone 77
- Creamy Avocado And White Bean Wrap 78
- Ravioli And Vegetable Pasta Soup 79
- Pearl Barley, Parsnip And Sage Rositto 80
- Porridge With Blueberry Compote 81
- Italian Vegetable Hoagies 82
- Spicy Root And Lentil Casserole 83
- Khoya Stuffed Matar Ki Tikki 84
- Vegetarian Biryani 85
- Marinated Aubergine And Rocket Salad 87
- Tofu Rancheros 88

Fontal Polenta With Mushroom Sauté 89

Cast Iron Fudge Brownies... 90

Apple Cobbler 91

Apple Brownie 93

Skillet Pecan Pie 94

Cast Iron Vanilla Cake 95

Chocolate Chip Skillet Cookie 97

Cast Iron Oatmeal Chocolate Cookie 98

Chocolate Skillet Cookie 99

Apple Skillet Cake..100

Fudge Skillet Cake 102

Cast Iron Almond Peach Tart..103

Apple Caramel Cake 105

Cast Iron Pineapple Skillet Sponge Cake.....................107

Peach Upside Down Cake..109

Caramel Chocolate Chip Cookie Cake 110

Conclusion 113

Part 1

Introduction

Do you have cast iron phobia? Are you afraid to use your cast iron skillet because you think it's hard to clean, temperamental and too much work?

Well, it's time for this madness to stop! Confront your cast iron phobia. Embrace your cast iron beauties. It's time for all voices to unite and proclaim, "I will no longer fear my cast iron skillet!"

This book is all about the proper way to care for and use your cast iron skillet. I'll show you how to clean it, season it, store it and cook in it. I'll tell you what seasoning is, and why it's important. I'll also give you some interesting cast iron history, and a few tips for finding used cast iron and restoring it. Plus, I'll get you started on a lifetime of cast iron cooking with some tried and true recipes.

I've had an (almost) lifelong romance with cast iron. It began around 1974, when my granny, Christine Greenwood Majure, taught me to make cornbread. Of course, I did play around with different types of cookware like non-stick Teflon® and stainless steel in my newlywed days. I even tried expensive enameled cast iron. But I always come back to my beloved cast iron pieces; not just my traditional skillets, but my griddle, my grill pan and a late addition called a Texas Skillet that I found at a yard sale in Los Angeles. Go figure.

Cast iron has survived in the kitchen jungle for so long because it's dependable. It's perfect for cooking so many things. It is the definition of easy care (no matter what you may think as you

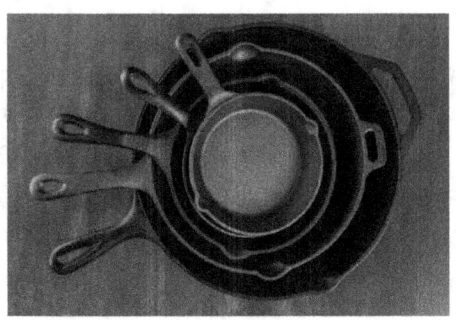

begin to read this little book) and if properly well-seasoned in the beginning, it will last several lifetimes—even if you occasionally abuse it and ignore it. It is a friend to outdoor cooks and indoor cooks alike. It will sear a steak to perfection at night and scramble fluffy eggs the next morning. It can press a Cuban sandwich and bake an apple pie. In a real pinch, it could well be your nearest and best defense against all forms of nefarious home intruder, giving you time to get away to safety and call the PoPo.

But I digress...

I hope you will take the hard-won information in this book and use it to divest yourself of your cast iron fear. Your cast iron pan wants to be used by you, loved by you. And if you let it, it will give you love in return, which you can then share with your family and friends. Now, isn't that what a faithful kitchen tool should do?

!6

As soon as you've finished reading this book, you'll have all the ammunition you need for a lifetime of cast iron care and cooking. You'll proudly raise your voice and say, "I am no longer afraid of my cast iron skillet!"

So, onward, oh ye of little cast iron experience. I'm about to arm you to the teeth with so much cast iron knowledge people will tell you to shut up about it, all while stuffing their faces with your delicious cast iron skillet creations.

!7

A Brief History of Cast Iron

Your beautiful cast iron skillet has a wonderful provenance. Cast iron has been around since about the 1st century BCE. The oldest examples have been discovered in China, where it was used to make everything from teapots to ploughs to ornamental pieces.

!8

Cast iron doesn't show up in the west until about the 16th century, when Henry VIII put it to good use for the Royal Navy. Cast iron was a cheap alternative to the forged steel and wrought iron typically used in weapons, so it was a frugal way to outfit a naval ship with weapons of war.

In 1707, a Quaker from Bristol, England, named Abraham Darby patented the first process for making thinner and lighter cast iron pots in blast furnaces. This revolutionized the market for cooking vessels, allowing nearly everyone to afford these time saving items.

Before the introduction of the first kitchen stoves in the mid-1700s, cast iron cook pots, like the cauldron, were used directly on the fire, and hailed as a (relatively) convenient way to cook a good meal for a hungry crowd. At that time, cast iron cooking pots were made with either a handle, so that they could be hung over the fire in a fireplace, or with three legs and a lid, called a spider, that could sit directly in the fire pit.

By the mid-19th century, flat-bottomed, legless pots like the Dutch oven were in use in households the world over. The skillet came along a bit later, and by the dawn of the 20th century, most households had at least one cast iron pan.

For nearly a century, the Griswold company, of Erie, Pennsylvania, established in 1865, and Wagner Ware of Sidney, Ohio, established in 1891, were the most popular purveyors of cast iron cookware in America.

A new comer, The Blacklock Foundry, later to become Lodge®, appeared on the scene in 1896. Owner Joseph Lodge created the iconic teardrop handle that is so closely associated with the Lodge® brand.

Lodge® is the only American cast iron cookware producing company in continuous operation since its founding. However, Griswold and Wagner Ware, both of which were bought by the Randall Corporation after their foundries initially folded in the 1950s, still produced some cast iron pieces through the 1990s, after being sold again to the General Housewares corporation. The American Culinary Corporation acquired both brands in 2000.

!9

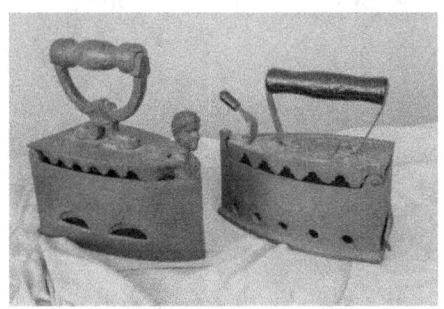

With the advent of modern cookware such as non-stick, Teflon®-coated cookware and enamel-coated cast iron cooking vessels like Le Creuset® in the 1960s and 1970s, the cast iron skillet fell out of favor and was relegated to yard sales and barn storage. The exception being avid campers who wanted to cook over an open fire and anyone who wanted to make crispy-crusted cornbread.

But cast iron is now having a resurgence in popularity. People are rediscovering the beauty of cast iron—not only its non-stick wonderfulness, but its collectibility, its usefulness, and its unique heritage. Vintage cast iron is seeing an unprecedented resurgence in interest, with some early and rare Griswold and Wagner Ware cast iron skillets going for as much as $2500

Today, there are many different types of cast iron cookware, everything from waffle irons and panini presses to grill pans. Cast iron may have gone in and out of vogue over the years, but good cooks always return to it because it's dependable and versatile. Cast iron is perfect for shaping, and over the many centuries of its use, its ability to retain heat for a long time has made it prized the world over for its perfect ability to sear and fry. When in doubt, cook it in your cast iron skillet. You just simply cannot go wrong when you cook in cast iron.

!10

What Is Seasoning?

Simply put, seasoning refers to the chemical process that occurs when a cast iron pan is coated with fat and heated for an extended period of time at a high temperature. By seasoning cast iron, you create a transformation of the fat used into a hardened polymer that protects the cast iron from rust. The fat literally hardens on the surface of the skillet, creating a moisture and oxygen barrier. The more layers of thin, hardened polymer applied to the cast iron pan, the better–and longer lasting–the barrier.

Cast iron is made up of a somewhat brittle metal alloy that contains a higher concentration of carbon than steel. It can be easily "cast" into a mold (or mould) to create objects. It is a porous metal (by that I mean it has pores, like your face, not that it has holes!) Oxidation, or rust, is caused when the pores of the iron are exposed to a combination of oxygen and moisture.

Coating the metal with a fat prevents moisture from reaching the metal, delaying the reaction that happens when iron is exposed to oxygen and moisture. When heated during the seasoning process, the fat seeps into the pores of the metal and seals them, creating a lasting barrier.

Strictly speaking, any fat or oil spread across the surface of an iron object, even if it isn't heated, will prevent rust in the short term. If you coat a bare cast iron pan with cooking oil and then store it in your pantry, for example, you will delay the onset of visible rust for a short period of time. It won't provide complete protection. Left unattended, you will see rust on your pan quickly.

!11

So there is a reason that we use a particular, and extended, process for seasoning a cast iron pan. The seasoning process produces a durable, hardened polymer finish that will protect your pan for a long, long, time. Possibly forever, if done right and continued over time. This allows the pan to be reliably used, even used every day, without worrying about removing rust before preparing food.

Seasoning has one other important function when it comes to a cast iron skillet: It creates a non-stick surface. If you have ever used an unseasoned cast iron pan, you know that when something sticks to it, it is the devil to remove it. It takes an intense amount of scrubbing to scrape off a stuck on grilled cheese, once it's bonded with an unseasoned cast iron pan. It can be done, of course, but it's not a fun process. Luckily, seasoning takes care of this problem.

I won't tell you that a well-seasoned pan is as slick as Teflon because it isn't. But, a well-seasoned cast iron pan is almost that slick. I've never had anything seriously stick to a pan that was well-seasoned. And even a moderately seasoned pan isn't hard to clean. Outside of the stuck on grilled cheese I mentioned above, a lightly seasoned pan will likely require a bit of elbow grease to remove some things—about the same amount of effort that you'd use to clean a gooey casserole dish.

So, now that you understand the reasons behind the seasoning process, you'll understand how important it is to the life of your pan, and why it isn't a step you'd want to skip.

!12

Don't Be Afraid of a New Cast

Iron Skillet

If you have just bought, or been given, a brand spanking new cast iron pan, you might be wondering what to do next.

Relax, that's what!

If you're like me, there is a certain excitement to bringing home a new kitchen pan or gadget. I always want to jump right in and try it out—see what it can do! But just as there are instructions to read with any new kitchen appliance, there are a few things you'll need to do to prepare your new cast iron pan for the seasoning process, and a few things to take note of before you begin. Don't let your enthusiasm get the better of you. Read this section carefully before you start the seasoning process.

A Few Things To Remember About A New Cast Iron Skillet One of the first things you might notice about a new cast iron skillet is that the color is a very dark grey or light black. To get the dark, deep, glossy black finish that means your skillet will shrug off even the stickiest cheese or the crustiest baked salmon, you're going to need to apply, and maintain, seasoning.

!13

Wait, you say! My pan is pre-seasoned! Can't I skip this step?

Sorry, hon, no.

It is important to remember that while your new pan probably does have a coating of some type of oil on it, it is not good enough, not by a long shot. This is the fatal flaw in those with good cast iron intentions, they skip the seasoning process when they get their new pan home.

The factory pre-seasoning process will temporarily prevent visible rust from forming on a new pan, but is not durable enough to prevent rust in the long term, nor prevent food from sticking .

Depending on which company manufactured your cast iron pan, the factory-based seasoning could be made up of industrial polymers (that you wouldn't want to end up in your food) and are used to retard the appearance of rust as the pan goes through many different climates.

Remember, rust on cast iron begins on a microscopic level long before it can be seen. And one thing you don't want to do is season a cast iron skillet over existing rust. This is not only a waste of time, it can permanently damage your pan.

!14

Some companies use a soy-based oil for factory seasoning, but some companies, specifically those that manufacture overseas, may use different types of industrial polymers, depending on where, and when, your pan was manufactured. Either way, it's best to start with a bare pan when beginning the seasoning process.

It may sound scary, all this talk about bare cast iron, stuck on food and industrial polymers, but don't be afraid. Take a breath, I'll walk you through it.

And, if you follow the **4 Easy Steps to Seasoning a Cast Iron Skillet** section of this book, and heed a few simple tips and tricks I will give you, you can use your new cast iron pan with confidence. In fact, the more you use it the better it gets, and the more you will want to use it.

When You Get Your New Pan Home

1. First, you need to wash your pan. This is one of only two times I will ever tell you to put soap on a cast iron pan, so make the most of it. Soap it up to your heart's content. It is important to wash a brand new pan to remove any industrial polymers, casting oils, dirt or dust that may be present before beginning the seasoning process.

2. Next, pat dry with a clean, soft kitchen towel.

3. Now, put your pan on the stove and turn the heat on medium. Allow your pan to heat until it shows no signs of dampness and begins to smoke slightly. (Turn your hood vent on, if desired.) This process may take up to 10 minutes. Do this to remove any trace of moisture, and to burn off any lingering smells from the casting process that may be present.

4. When your pan is completely dry, hot, and smoking slightly, turn the stove off and allow your pan to cool completely on the stovetop. DO NOT ATTEMPT TO HANDLE OR

MOVE YOUR PAN WITHOUT HEAT RESISTANT OVEN MITTS OR HEAT

RESISTANT GLOVES! Your pan is scalding hot and serious burns could result.

!15

Following the 4 steps above do 3 things: 1. A good washing with soap and hot water will remove any dirt, oil or industrial polymers that are on your pan.

2. Heating your pan on the stove ensures that your pan is completely dry, which is important for the seasoning process to work effectively.

3. Heating until the pan smokes slightly burns off any chemical odors that may be present.

This step isn't strictly necessary, I guess, but I do it because I don't like any off-smelling odors attaching to something I might cook.

You will probably never need to repeat these steps, unless you get another new cast iron pan, of course. But, should you ever have a question about whether or not your pan has residual moisture, it's a good way to make sure your pan is always completely dry before storage. Plus, it's a great way to remove any lingering food odors, such as those that might be present after cooking fish. (More on this in the Tips and Tricks section) A Note About Heating A Cast Iron Pan

Why does it take so long for cast iron to heat up? Because cast iron is not a particularly good conductor of heat, it can take a while for the entire pan to become throughly heated. Copper or stainless steel are much better choices if quick heating is what you're after in a cooking vessel. But, even though cast iron takes a while to completely heat up means that cast iron stays hot for a very long time. This is one of the reasons cast iron is so good for searing and frying.

But remember, just because a cast iron pan takes a long time to completely heat, doesn't mean that it isn't hot to the touch.

CAUTION!

Always exercise caution when dealing with a hot (or heating) cast iron pan. Use heat resistant pot holders or gloves when handling a hot cast iron pan.

!16

Don't Be Afraid of a Used Cast

Iron Skillet, Either!

Is it okay to buy a used cast iron skillet? Of Course!

A used cast iron pan can be a great discovery and a wonderful addition to your kitchen. Never worry about buying or being given an old pan. The only thing you'll need to decide is whether it is a pan that can be used for cooking or if it will be decorative.

For the most part, there is never a problem with reclaiming and cooking in a used cast iron pan—many can be restored with a few simple steps and go on to continue their beautiful cast iron destiny in your care. In fact, cast iron is probably one of the only collectibles that is actually designed to be used, even after purchase. The cooking surface of a cast iron skillet will just keep getting better and better, even after 100 years—if it hasn't been neglected to the point of ruin, of course.

When cared for properly, cast iron is nearly indestructible, and a great value for the money.

Even if you find a pan that is dirty and gunky, even if there is extensive visible rust, 9 times out of 10 it can still be restored and used.

A vintage cast iron pan is a true treasure. Vintage pans are more well-made that today's cast iron. For one thing, they are thinner and lighter than more modern cast iron pans, and the

!17

cooking surface of vintage pans was probably hand-polished, making it smoother, and allowing for a deeper and glossier seasoned surface, which translates into a better non-stick surface.

The downside is that vintage pans are hard to find and are pricier. Expect to pay between $50

and $200 for average vintage skillets. The older and rarer the pan, the more expensive your purchase will be. Rare skillets from Griswold and Wagner Ware are often seen priced in the $1000s.

If you're looking to collect vintage cast iron, it's worth reading up on trademarks and styles, so you know what you're looking for, and what those pieces should be worth. I'm not well-versed enough in truly collectible vintage cast iron to tell you what to look for, but there are many experts out there who can.

That being said, I wouldn't shy away from buying a more modern cast iron thrift store find. It might be newer, and it might take a bit more seasoning, but in the end you can create the smooth, glossy, black finish that careful seasoning will produce. I've found "modern" cast iron skillets at garage sales for about $3. What a bargain!

What To Look For In A Used Cast Iron Pan

There are 2 types of damage to be aware of when looking at used cast iron pans; serious and surface. It might take a bit of practice, but you can learn to spot the difference.

Serious damage, just as it sounds, will impair the function of the pan. It's probably best to avoid a pan with serious damage, especially if it is your first cast iron pan. While it's likely you can restore some of its beauty with attention and care, a pan with serious damage is not one you'll want to cook in.

Surface damage, on the other hand, even if it looks bad, isn't. This is a pan that can be repaired. You can clean and re-season your pan and it can go on to serve you well in the years ahead.

!18

Keep These Tips In Mind When Choosing A Used Pan

Examine the pan for structural damage.

What you want to avoid is breakage, such as a broken handle, cracked cooking surface, or warping. This type of damage will impair the function of the pan, and your ability to season and clean it properly. With this type of damage, there may well be serious (structural) rust damage as well, even if you can't see it.

Examine the pan for rust damage.

Most, if not all, used pans will have some rust. Oxidation is a normal state for a neglected cast iron pan. Don't worry too much about how much of the pan is rusted, or even if the entire surface is covered in rust. What you should do is touch the rust. Does it come off easily with your fingers and appear only on the top layer of the pan? Is the cooking surface flaking off?

Avoid rust that goes deeply into the metal, especially if there is any sign of flaking or crumbling metal.

!20

Examine the pan for pitting or holes in the metal.

Avoid a pan with rust or damage that has caused a hole anywhere in the metal, or a pitted look to the cooking surface. This type of damage is not repairable. If you love this pan, use it for decorative purposes only, and be aware that the pan may continue to deteriorate.

Don't try to "season over" any kind of serious cast iron damage, like that listed above.

It won't stop the rust from eating away at your pan, and your pan will never look nor perform the way you'd want it to.

What if the pan has nicks and scratches?

A slightly banged-up cast iron pan, full of surface nicks in the seasoning, or even small, superficial chips and scratches in the seasoning is okay, as long as there isn't serious rust damage. This pan is still a treasure.

Surface rust isn't a problem!

As stated before, rust is almost a given for a used cast iron pan. Surface rust, especially rust that can be wiped off easily with your finger is perfectly acceptable.

A used cast iron skillet makes a great gift!

Remember that a used cast iron pan makes a great gift, especially if you season the pan well before gifting it! Fill it with cast iron skillet necessities like Crisco®, a good brush for cleaning, sturdy pot holders and some recipes, or even a copy of this book, and you'll have a wonderful gift that will be treasured for years to come.

!21

How to Reclaim a Cast Iron Pan

If you're buying an old cast iron skillet, you will have to deal with removing rust and old seasoning build up before you begin to re-season your pan, and there are a number of ways to go about this.

Depending on the amount of rust, old seasoning and good ol' gunk you're dealing with, you might have to use several different methods to remove it all. I've found that starting out with the least caustic method and progressing toward the most severe is the way to go, that way you can stop the minute you see that the rust and old seasoning has been removed. It lets you get to the re-seasoning process as soon as possible, while not inflicting damage to your pan. A win-win.

One quick disclaimer here: I am not an expert on collecting priceless vintage cast iron. When I write about reclaiming cast iron, I am talking about vintage pans that you might find at an estate sale or garage sale that you would like to use yourself or display in your home. If you want to try collecting truly rare vintage cast iron collectibles, please do your own research, and seek out the knowledge of those much more well-versed in ways to maintain the integrity of your pan.

Any method used to remove old seasoning and rust could potentially cause damage to a collectible cast iron pan, which could alter its value.

4 WAYS TO RECLAIM A CAST IRON SKILLET

Steel Wool Method #1

Start here to remove rust and old seasoning. This is an almost no-fail way to clean rust off old cast iron. Scrub the entire pan, inside and out.

What You'll Need

- Steel Wool Cleaning Pads such as Brillo® or SOS®

Instructions

1. Wet the steel wool cleaning pad and use it to scrub all areas of the pan until rust and old seasoning is removed. Since the steel wool cleaning pad already has soap in it, when you've removed the rust and old seasoning just rinse well with warm water.

2. Inspect your pan for remaining rust, or any unseen damage.

3. If there is none, then place pan on stove over medium heat until thoroughly dry.

4. Beginning with a cool pan, proceed with the seasoning process as instructed.

Steel Wool Method #2

This method is good for removing rust that's heavier or covers a larger percentage of your pan.

What You'll Need:

- Cooking Oil

- Commercial Grade Steel Wool, grades 0-Medium Fine to 4-Extra Coarse, depending on the amount of rust on your pan. (This is available at your local hardware store. Ask your hardware store sales staff for guidance, if needed.)

!23

Instructions

1. Pour some cooking oil into your pan.

2. Use the steel wool to scrub the rusty areas of your pan first, then scrub all areas of your pan, inside and out. You may have to repeat the process several times. Start with the finest grade of commercial steel wool and increase the texture grade as needed until the rust and old seasoning is removed.

3. Rinse pan throughly and inspect for unseen damage.

4. Wash your pan thoroughly with soap and hot water.

5. Dry with a clean kitchen towel, and put on your stove on medium heat until your pan is completely dry.

6. Beginning with a cool pan, proceed with the seasoning process as instructed.

The Oven Cleaner Method

I think this is a drastic method, and I'd only use it if steel wool scrubbing didn't do the trick.

The reason this method works is based on the main ingredient in oven cleaner, which is lye.

Soaking cast iron in a lye bath will effectively remove both rust and seasoning, but few of us have access to a tub of lye large enough to soak cookware in, so oven cleaner seems the next best solution. But improperly done, this method might cause damage to your pan. It's also time consuming and messy. Only use this method while outside, both for good ventilation and the fact that oven cleaner might damage countertops and other kitchen furnishings. Keep this project well away from children and pets, as oven cleaner is caustic. Choose an oven cleaner product with the highest concentration of lye for best results.

What You'll Need:

• Oven Cleaner

• Rubber Gloves

• Protective eyewear such as goggles

• Face Mask

• Plastic Bag Large Enough To Fully Enclose Pan

• Heavy Duty tape or a zip tie, to completely close plastic bag

!24

Instructions

1. First, wipe any dust or debris out of your pan. Make sure it is thoroughly dry before you begin.

2. Next, while in a well-ventilated area, and wearing a face mask, goggles and rubber gloves, coat your pan throughly with the oven cleaner.

3. Put the oven cleaner-coated pan in the plastic bag and seal it completely using tape or zip ties. Put it in a warm place, such as outside in the sun, and leave it for 24 hours.

4. After 24 hours, and while wearing rubber gloves, goggles and a face mask, open the plastic bag and check the pan to see if the rust and seasoning has been removed. If it has, remove the pan, and while still wearing rubber gloves, wash the pan well with warm soapy water.

5. If it hasn't been completely removed, re-close the plastic bag and leave the pan in a warm place for another 24 hours. Alternately, you can rinse and dry the pan to assess the amount of rust and seasoning that remains. If your pan still needs work, put on rubber gloves, goggles and a face mask, and re-coat the pan with oven cleaner. Insert into a new plastic bag and seal. Leave in a warm spot for another 24 hours.

6. Do not leave the pan in the plastic bag coated in oven cleaner for longer than a total of 48 hours. If you do, it could destroy

your pan. At the end of no more than 48 hours, remove the pan and wash thoroughly in warm soapy water.

7. You can use a steel wool soap pad such as SOS® or Brillo®, or commercial grade steel wool as outlined above, to remove any lingering rust.and seasoning Do not use any more oven cleaner on your pan.

8. When ready, clean your pan with soap and warm water. Put the pan on the stove over medium heat until completely dry.

9. Then, beginning with a cool pan, proceed with the seasoning process as instructed.

!25

Self-Cleaning Oven Method

I'm going to put a disclaimer on this method, too. This is the method of last resort. You run the risk of ruining your pan if you do this. Your pan could crack or warp if this method is used, so beware! I wouldn't use this method on a pan that is considered valuable, such as a family keepsake or collectible.

What You'll Need:

• Self-Cleaning Oven

Instructions

1. Here's how: Put your pan in the oven and set to self-clean. Leave in the oven until the entire cycle is over. Allow pan to cool completely before removing from the oven. Your pan should emerge stripped down to the bare metal.

2. If you do this, you'll need to turn around and start the seasoning process on your pan right away. A pan that is stripped to the bare metal has absolutely no protection from oxidation. Season immediately using steps outlined in this book.

!26

How to Season a Cast Iron Pan

When it comes to seasoning a cast iron pan, it doesn't matter if it's new, old, vintage or ancient, the steps are always the same. The only thing that matters is that you go through the steps in the order they are listed, and that you repeat them often enough that your pan becomes well-seasoned.

After your pan is prepared according to the instructions for either a new or reclaimed pan, go through the seasoning instructions in this section in exactly the order stated. Repeat until your pan is glossy, slick and black. This will take a while to complete, so don't wait until the seasoning process is complete before you start using your pan. You can (and should) use it while going through the seasoning process. It's okay to take your time with seasoning. It really doesn't have to be completed in one day. You have, literally, a lifetime to season and use your pan.

But also remember, a lightly seasoned pan will not perform like a well-seasoned pan. To limit your frustration with stuck on messes and ensure the durability of your pan, it's best to get at least one seasoning layer on your pan as quickly as possible. The more you use your pan, whether that is through baking cornbread or frying fish, the better the seasoning will be. If you use your pan often, you'll be building seasoning without really working too hard at it, even though you'll need to continue the formal seasoning steps below as well. Think of it like you would servicing your car—it's routine maintenance. Even after your pan is very well-seasoned, a couple times a year, repeat the seasoning steps. Just think of it as a tune-up for your pan.

!27

Season Any Cast Iron Skillet In 4 Easy Steps After preparing your pan according to instructions for either a new or reclaimed pan, follow the instructions below.

1. Set your oven to 400 degrees. Allow it to preheat completely.

2. Wash and dry your hands throughly. Then, using your FINGERS, coat your pan with a very small amount (1/8 teaspoon) of solid vegetable shortening, like Crisco®. Coat every nook and cranny, inside and out, with the shortening. Pay special attention to the cooking surface and lip of your pan. It should be a very light coating, but one that completely covers the entire pan.

3. Put your pan in the oven, right side up, and bake for 1 hour. Don't open the oven door.

4. After 1 hour, turn the oven off and allow your pan to cool completely while in the oven.

When cool, your pan is ready to use!

How easy is that? Now you are on your way to a perfectly seasoned cast iron skillet!

A word about the amount of shortening to use when seasoning your cast iron skillet...

Seasoning works best when it is built up over time from very thin layers of hardened polymer.

Applying excess shortening will not get you the desired result faster, it will only cause your seasoning to be uneven, and possibly flake off during cooking or cleaning. Even if you think 1/8 teaspoon of Crisco won't be enough to cover your skillet, wait and see before adding more.

I've found that even a very large Dutch oven and lid can be coated with 1/2 teaspoon or so of Crisco. If the surface of your pan has a pooling, oily slick, you have applied to much shortening.

!28

Uneven seasoning caused by excess fat in your skillet could cause your pan to have areas of unseasoned iron that could begin to rust underneath a later seasoning layer, which could ultimately destroy your pan. The seasoning process will be repeated over and over, so there is no need to rush it or hurry it. You have plenty of time—a lifetime—to season and use your pan.

So remember, less is more when it comes to the amount of fat used and the seasoning process.

See the **Tips &Tricks Section** for more info on the amount and type of fat to use during seasoning of your cast iron skillet.

!29

How to Clean a Cast Iron Pan

Cleaning your cast iron pan is just as important as seasoning it. But don't worry, it's not as hard a job as you may have been led to believe. Follow the instructions below and you'll have a spotless pan, ready for your next delicious cast iron skillet creation.

4 Steps to a Sparkling Cast Iron Skillet

1. First, run hot water on your pan to loosen any food particles.

2. Next, (with hot water running or not, your choice) use a stiff brush and a circular motion to scrub the cooking surface of your pan. Be careful not to gouge the surface as this will damage the seasoning. Rinse well with hot water after scrubbing.

3. It is not necessary to use soap on your pan. Hot water and a stiff brush should remove any food residue from your pan. (See Tips & Tricks section for how to remove a stuck on mess without soap.)

4. When your pan is clean, use a clean kitchen towel to thoroughly dry it. At this point, you can store your skillet, or continue the seasoning process as instructed.

If you feel your pan is not completely dry:

1. Put it on the stove over medium heat for a few minutes to dry out, 2. Or put your pan in a warm oven for a few minutes to dry out. Either way, make sure your pan is completely dry before storage.

!30

Why Is the Brush I Use to Clean My Pan Important?

Almost any non-metal brush will do, but I use a brush that is meant to scrub vegetables. I prefer the vegetable brush because it's sturdy, can go in the dishwasher and is round, which allows me to get into all the curves of my pan.

Kitchen Aid® makes a very good vegetable brush, which costs about $6. Lodge® also makes a round brush with a long handle that is specifically designed for cleaning cast iron pans, so that could be a good choice as well. You might have to experiment to find what works best for you and your pans.

Choosing a Brush to Clean Your Cast Iron Skillet

1. Choose a stiff, non-metal brush, such as a vegetable brush, to clean your cast iron pan.

Choose a round brush over a square one, so you can reach all the curves of your pan.

2. You could also use the green side of a Scotch-Brite® scrubby sponge or a plastic sponge designed for use with Teflon® non-stick pans, without soap.

3. Never use a brush designed for cleaning grills, or any kind of steel wool, SOS® or Brillo® Pads for regular cleaning of your cast iron pan.

4. Be careful not to gouge the surface of the pan as you scrub, as this can damage the seasoning.

Use a gently, circular motion when cleaning your skillet. Remember, a well-seasoned pan will take a more through scrubbing than a lightly seasoned skillet. You don't want to remove any of the seasoning from your pan when cleaning.

!31

Tips & Tricks for a Lifetime of

Cast Iron Use

Here are a few important tips to remember, now that you're on your way to a well-seasoned pan.

1. A good time to season your pans is in the evening after dinner, so you can let them cool in the oven overnight.

2. Never, ever, under any circumstances, allow your pan to soak in water. Not for any amount of time. It is a recipe for a rusted pan, even if it is well-seasoned.

3. If you can't clean your pan right away, just let it sit on the stove or in the oven until you can get to it. But don't go off and leave it soaking in the sink.

4. Whether your pan is new or re-claimed, until it is very well-seasoned, add a small amount (1/16 teaspoon or so) of Crisco® to the pan each time you use it.

5. Adding a small amount of shortening to the pan each time you use it doesn't take the place of other fats, like butter or olive oil, that you might want to add for cooking purposes.

Whether you're scrambling eggs, making cornbread or cooking chili, simply adding a tiny bit of Crisco® to the pan while it's heating, and letting it melt and spread across the cooking surface, will make a huge difference in the durability of your seasoning. Every time you do

!32

this, you're gently continuing the seasoning process and helping to build up that glossy black non-stick finish. You will quickly notice an improvement in your pan when you do this one thing.

After the shortening has melted, and while using a potholder to hold your pan, tip the pan and allow the shortening to spread across the cooking surface. Then add whatever additional fat you wish, such as butter or oil. You can also continue cooking without adding any other fat.

This is a small amount of shortening, and shouldn't add significantly to the fat calories of whatever you're cooking.

!33

Cast Iron FAQ

Q:

Why use my fingers when putting shortening on my pan when seasoning it?

A:

Using your fingers will allow you to feel every nook, cranny and groove of your pan, which means a more thorough coating of fat, and thereby a more complete seasoning. Using your fingers will allow you to spread the shortening across your pan in the thinnest layer possible. Also, you'll be able to feel the seasoning as it builds. This will help you notice any spots on your pan that may need extra attention.

Q:

Why can't I use a paper towel to coat my pan with shortening?

A:

Over the years, I've found that paper towels can leave behind tiny paper fibers and particles that interfere with the seasoning process. I think clean fingers do a better job, and there's no risk of leaving bits of paper behind that could flake off into your food or catch fire at high heat.

Q:

Can't I use olive oil or canola oil or avocado oil when seasoning my pan?

A:

There are many books and websites that will tell you to use whatever oil you have on hand, including olive oil, to season your cast iron skillet. Don't do it.

!34

Here's why:

1. The smoke point of many oils, such as olive oil, is very low. Using it can produce a smoky mess in a 400 degree oven. The temperature of your oven must be high enough to polymerize the fat, and create the seasoning layer you want. The smoke point of shortening is about 500 degrees, well above the temperature needed to create the polymerization.

2. Vegetable oils like canola oil can sometimes produce a sticky residue on your pan—no matter how often you repeat the seasoning process. This can cause food to stick to your pan, and make cleaning difficult.

3. I've heard people say that they use bacon grease when seasoning a cast iron pan. I don't, even though bacon grease should work in roughly the same way as shortening. But bacon grease can turn rancid, and I personally don't like to take the chance. My granny used lard, which worked well when she seasoned her cast iron, and you can still find it at any Wal-Mart. But lard, like bacon grease, turns rancid at room temperature.

Crisco®, on the other hand, is shelf-stable, widely available, and there is no worry about cooking eggs in a pan that's seasoning has turned rancid.

4. Pans I have seasoned with solid vegetable shortening have no sticky residue, seem to have a more durable finish, gain non-stick properties more quickly, and look glossy and black more quickly than the pans where I have used liquid oil.

Q:

Food is sticking to my new pan! Help!

A:

After cooking in a new or lightly seasoned pan, you might notice some mild food sticking. This is normal until the glossy black non-stick finish is achieved. Don't worry, it's completely normal at this point in your cast iron's life. I find the worst culprits are eggs and cheese, so you might want to avoid these foods until your pan has a good level of seasoning.

After you build up a good seasoning layer, you shouldn't have any trouble with these items at all. But if you do find that you can't get your pan clean with just hot water and a stiff brush, don't worry, there is a simple solution.

!35

Put enough very hot tap water in your pan to cover the stuck on mess. Put your pan on the stove and bring the water to a boil over medium heat. Using a wooden or silicon spatula or spoon, gently rub and scrap the stuck on food until it is removed. When your pan has cooled enough to handle, rinse your pan in very hot tap water, scrubbing with the stiff brush, if needed, and dry as usual. Voila! A sparkling pan.

Q:

Where do I store my pan when I'm not using it?

A:

I store my pans in the oven, the way my granny taught me. Some people say that you can store a cast iron pan in your pantry, and theoretically you can, but there are two things to consider:

1. Cast iron pans are heavy, so storing them in the pantry or in a kitchen cabinet could warp or even break a shelf, especially if you have several pans nested together.

2. Storing pans in the pantry might allow rust to get a toe-hold, even on a well-seasoned pan if it isn't used for a while. I've never found rust on a pan that was stored in my oven, even if it's been a long time since I've used it.

3. The oven is arguably the driest spot in your kitchen. Plus, when you use your oven and return your pan to it afterward, you ensure that there is no moisture on or around the pan. This helps to remove any risk of rust.

Q:

Why dry my pan on the stovetop?

A:

Again, this is simply to make sure that your pan is completely dry before storage. But I find there is another reason that I like to do it: Heating the pan on the stove for a few minutes after use will burn off any cooking odors that might remain, ensuring that the next time you scramble eggs, they don't taste like fried fish!

!36

Q:

Isn't skipping soap unsanitary?

A:

I've never used soap on my cast iron pans and I've never had an issue. Begin and maintain a thorough and well-seasoned pan, and hot water and a stiff brush should be all you need.

Q:

I can't stand it, I MUST use soap on my pan.

A:

I know people who feel this way. I don't agree with them, but I respect their feelings. I will just say this, if you insist on using soap on your cast iron skillet, you may be removing some of the seasoning each time you do, which will make forming and maintaining a good seasoning harder. And if you insist on using soap, NEVER USE DAWN® on your cast iron pan. That is no slap against Dawn®, it is a great product—for cutting through baked on grease, which is what your cast iron seasoning layer is made up of. If you remove the seasoning layer (which is made up of a heat-hardened fat) you are stripping your pan each time you wash it. If you feel you must use soap on your cast iron pan, use the mildest dish soap you can find, and use it sparingly.

Q:

Shouldn't I turn my pan upside down in the oven when I season it?

A:

The prevailing wisdom of this procedure is that you turn the pan upside down to allow the excess fat to drip out of the pan and onto a cookie sheet below. This is a mystery to me because the whole point of baking the fat-coated pan in the oven is that the fat stays on the pan and hardens. How can the fat stay on the pan if the pan is upside-down?

But, if you apply only a very thin layer of shortening to your pan as part of the seasoning process, there is no need to turn your pan upside down because there will be no pooling or dripping of the fat, thus no need to have an area on which to let it drip. Plus, all that dripping fat in a 400 degree oven is just a recipe for smoke and possible fire. Better to stick to a very thin layer of shortening and be done. As an added bonus, you won't have to clean your oven or your oven racks every time you season your skillet.

!37

Q:

Can I cook tomatoes or other acidic foods in my cast iron pan?

A:

Yes, and no. After your pan is well-seasoned, it is fine to cook tomatoes or other acidic foods in it without fear. But before you have a well-seasoned pan, I'd avoid it. Acidic foods can react with a cast iron pan, causing an off, metallic taste. Once your pan is well-seasoned, your pan is protected from the damage that acidic foods can cause, because the seasoning layer is between the metal and the food. Even after seasoning, though, I'd be careful about leaving foods like spaghetti sauce or chili in my cast iron pan for long periods. And never store food (especially acidic foods) in a cast iron pan. Any moisture, especially from acidic foods, can eventually break down the seasoning of your pan.

Cast Iron Recipes

Now that you've read all about how to season and care for your cast iron skillet, it's time to try it out! Cooking in cast iron is one of the most rewarding experiences you will ever have in the kitchen. Your cast iron skillet is dependable and can be the cornerstone of your cooking repertoire. I've included a few simple recipes to get you started on a lifetime of delicious cast iron cooking.

Cast Iron Chi-Town Deep Dish Skillet Pizza

My family loves deep dish Chicago-style pizza, and this easy recipe allows us to have it any time we want, without the airline ticket! Use sliced mozzarella instead of shredded for an authentic taste. Serves 4.

Ingredients:

- 1 Container refrigerated pizza dough

- 1 teaspoon sugar

- 1 15 oz can diced tomatoes, very well drained

- 1 teaspoon oregano

- 2 oz crushed tomato purée

- 1 teaspoon basil

- 1 6 oz. package sliced pepperoni

- 2 cloves garlic, minced

- 24 oz good quality mozzarella, sliced

- Vegetable shortening, like Crisco

- 4 oz good quality shaved or shredded

- Red pepper flakes, salt and pepper, to taste

Parmesan

!40

Instructions:

1. Preheat your oven to 400 degrees. Throughly grease bottom and sides of an 8" cast iron skillet with shortening. Remove pizza crust from package and unroll. Gently stretch the pizza crust to fit the bottom of your skillet, pushing into the curve of the pan to make a

"corner." Continue to push the pizza dough up the sides of the skillet to the lip of the pan, aiming for a uniform thickness. You may have to trim some areas and add the dough to others to completely cover the skillet. Allow it to rest for about 5 minutes.

2. Meanwhile, drain tomatoes well and put in a medium bowl. Add crushed tomatoes, sugar, garlic, oregano, basil, salt, pepper and red pepper flakes. Mix well and set aside.

3. Bake pizza dough in oven for about 10 minutes, until it is beginning to brown and puffs slightly. Remove crust from oven. Leave oven on.

4. Layer half of the sliced mozzarella over the crust, fanning toward the outer edge, but covering the crust completely. Next, layer on half of the pepperoni slices. Add another layer of

mozzarella, and another layer of pepperoni. End with a last layer of mozzarella.

5. Scatter the diced tomato mixture over the mozzarella, then sprinkle the parmesan over the tomatoes. Bake for 15-18 minutes, or until the crust is brown and crisp, and the cheese is melted and bubbly. Remove from oven and allow to rest for 10 minutes before slicing and serving.

The key to making this dish is layering the ingredients in the order they are listed. Putting the tomatoes on top ensures a crisp crust, but you can personalize your pizza anyway you like!

Replace the pepperoni with cooked sausage, bacon, ground beef, or ham. Go all veg with green and red peppers, mushrooms, olives, and onions, or simply add a layer of vegetables in place of a layer of meat. Substitute sliced cheddar or provolone for all or part of the mozzarella—the combinations are endless. If using canned items like mushrooms or olives, drain very well before adding to the pizza to avoid a soggy-bottomed crust.

!41

Cast Iron Thin Crust Caprese Skillet Pizza

This is an easy and delicious appetizer, reminiscent of bruschetta, but with a cracker-like crust. Goes well with a good glass of wine. Serves 6.

Ingredients:

- 1 Container refrigerated thin-crust pizza

- 1 8 oz container fresh mozzarella

dough

- 2 teaspoons minced garlic

- 24. oz fresh grape tomatoes, washed and

- 1 8 oz container refrigerated fresh pesto

halved

sauce

- 10 fresh basil leaves, shredded

- Salt and freshly ground black pepper to

- 3 tablespoons olive oil

taste

!42

Ingredients:

1. Preheat oven to 400 degrees.

2. Using a pastry brush, coat a 12 inch cast iron skillet with about 2 teaspoons of olive oil.

3. Add pizza dough to skillet, using fingers to push and stretch dough to fit bottom of pan, trimming as needed to fit. Dough should be thin, but not so thin that there are holes in the dough. Using a fork, prick the crust several times, to prevent air bubbles from forming as the crust bakes.

4. Drizzle 1 tablespoon of olive oil over top of crust. Lightly salt and pepper crust, if desired. Bake crust for 10-15 minutes, or until it is browned, crisp, and cooked through.

5. While crust is baking, add remaining 2 tablespoons of olive oil to an 8 inch cast iron skillet, and heat over medium heat until oil begins to shimmer.

6. Add garlic and sauté quickly, until the garlic becomes fragrant, about 1 minute.

7. Reduce heat to low and add grape tomatoes, cooking gently and stirring mixture, until the tomatoes begin to blister and pop, about 3-4 minutes.

8. Remove pan from heat and add salt and pepper to taste.

9. When crust is ready, remove from oven.

10. Next, spread pesto over warm crust. Slice fresh mozzarella thinly, and layer over pesto, adding salt and pepper if desired.

11. Top with tomato mixture and shredded basil leaves. Slice and enjoy!

12. If the residual heat from the crust is not enough to melt the mozzarella, put the skillet back in the oven for 1-2 minutes to allow the cheese to melt before serving.

!43

Cast Iron Easy Focaccia

This quick recipe goes great with a salad or as a complement to a heartier meal. Serves 4.

Ingredients:

- 1 Container refrigerated pizza dough
- Fresh Thyme leaves
- 1 6 oz can sliced black olives, well drained
- Sea salt and freshly ground pepper to taste
- 1 tablespoon olive oil
- Fresh Rosemary
- Shredded Asiago cheese

!44

Instructions:

1. Preheat oven to 375 degrees.

2. Cut pizza dough in half, reserving remaining half for another use.

3. Use a pastry brush to lightly coat an 8 inch cast iron skillet with about 1 teaspoon of olive oil.

4. Add pizza dough to skillet, using fingers to push and stretch the dough to fit. Dough will be slightly thick. Use the round end of a wooden spoon to gently make several indentations in the dough. Don't press all the way through the dough.

5. Scatter black olives over dough, then sprinkle dough with sea salt, fresh pepper, fresh rosemary leaves and thyme leaves. Top with Asiago cheese. Drizzle with remaining olive oil.

6. Bake 10-15 minutes, or until slightly puffed and golden brown. Let rest 5 minutes before serving.

7. Make it special! Before drizzling with olive oil, scatter sun dried tomatoes, and sliced green olives over dough. Proceed as directed.

!45

Cast Iron New Orleans Pain Perdu

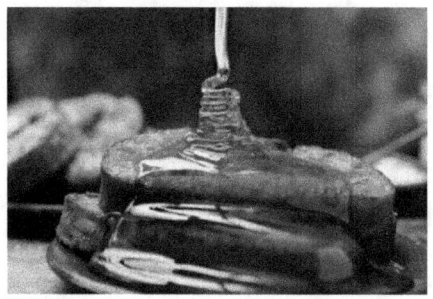

Pan Perdu is a delicious New Orleans-style French Toast treat, made here with a cast iron spin. French for "lost bread," this recipe works best with very stale French bread, so if your bread isn't quite stale yet, slice it into 2 inch pieces and let it sit uncovered on the counter overnight. Serves 4.

Ingredients:

- 1/2 cup whole milk

- 1/8 teaspoon Allspice

- 1/2 cup half and half

- 1/8 teaspoon Nutmeg

- 2 eggs, well beaten

- 2 tablespoons butter

- 1 tsp vanilla

- 2 tablespoons vegetable oil

- Pinch salt

- 8 slices stale French bread, (about 2 inches

- 6 tablespoons sugar, divided

thick)

- 1/2 teaspoon cinnamon

- Syrup or confectioner's sugar for serving

!46

1. Mix first 5 ingredients, plus 3 tablespoons sugar, together in a large, deep bowl.

2. Add stale French bread slices and turn several times to coat. Allow bread to soak in milk mixture until all liquid is absorbed. (Alternately, you can cover the mixture with plastic wrap and let it sit in the refrigerator overnight.)

3. Mix remaining 3 tablespoons of sugar with the cinnamon, allspice and nutmeg, set aside.

4. When you are ready to cook the Pain Perdu, preheat oven to 375 degrees.

5. Add the butter and oil to a 12 inch cast iron skillet, and heat over medium heat until hot.

6. Add the bread slices to the skillet and cook for about 2 minutes.

7. Flip bread slices over and sprinkle with the sugar/cinnamon mixture.

8. Put the skillet in the oven and continue cooking for 10-12 minutes, until the Pain Perdu is golden brown and the sugar mixture is caramelized.

9. Remove from oven and serve immediately with syrup, or sprinkled with powdered sugar.

!47

Cast Iron Skillet Fried Chicken Tenders

With Creamy Peppered Gravy

Is there anything better than fried chicken? Nope—especially when it's served with this creamy, peppery gravy. It's based on a recipe handed down from my husband's grandfather, and delicious served with french fries, mashed potatoes, or for a real treat, buttermilk biscuits, so you don't miss a drop. Serves 4-6

!48

Ingredients:

- 2 large chicken tenderloins, cut into 2 inch
- 1 cup half and half

strips

- 1/2 cup chicken stock
- 1 2/3 cups all-purpose flour, divided
- 1 teaspoon salt, plus more for gravy, if
- 2 eggs, well beaten

needed

- 4 cups milk, divided
- 1 1/2 teaspoons pepper, divided
- 1-2 shakes hot sauce, like Tabasco, or to
- 1-2 cups oil, or enough to reach about a 2

taste

inch depth in your skillet when heated.

Instructions

1. In a 12 inch cast iron skillet, heat oil over medium heat until hot and shimmering.

2. Meanwhile, in a large bowl, mix 1 1/3 cups flour with 1 teaspoon salt and 1/2 teaspoon pepper. Set aside.

3. In another bowl, mix 1 cup of milk with a shake or two of the hot sauce.

4. Working with one hand as a "dry" hand, and one hand as a "wet" hand, dredge chicken pieces first in the flour mixture, then in the milk mixture, then back into the flour mixture. Shake off excess flour and put immediately into hot oil.

5. Fry chicken in batches, turning once, about 4 minutes per strip, or until golden and cooked through, and until all chicken is fried.

6. Remove skillet from heat. Remove all but 1 tablespoon oil from the pan, but leaving any crunchy pieces of chicken in the bottom of the skillet.

7. Return skillet to low heat and add the remaining 1/3 cup of flour, stirring to combine with the oil in the skillet. Cook, stirring constantly, until the flour mixture is smooth and bubbling, but before it begins to brown.

8. Slowly add the chicken stock and stir until smooth, scraping up any browned bits, then add the remaining milk and half and half. Cook gravy, stirring frequently until bubbly and thickened. Add remaining 1 teaspoon pepper. Taste and add salt, if desired.

If gravy thickens too much, thin with additional milk or chicken stock, until desired consistency.

9. Serve hot over fried chicken strips.

!49

Southern Skillet Cornbread

This recipe is based on my granny's original recipe. It makes a very "short" cornbread—

meaning it is thin, with a very crisp crust and fluffy center. For a truly southern treat, crumble a cornbread wedge into a glass, top with either sweet milk or buttermilk, and eat with a spoon.

Add a slice of onion, and people will think you were born in the South—even if you don't say

"y'all." Serves 4-6.

!50

Ingredients:

- 1 1/2 C. Yellow or White Cornmeal
- 1/4 C. Oil
- 1/2 C. Self-rising Flour
- 1 Egg
- 1/2 C. (more or less) milk or buttermilk
- Crisco

Instructions:

1. Preheat oven to 400 degrees.

2. Thoroughly, but not heavily, grease an 8" cast iron skillet.

3. Put skillet in oven to heat while you mix cornbread ingredients. Be sure to allow the skillet to heat throughly before carefully removing from the oven.

4. While your skillet heats, combine all dry ingredients in a bowl.

5. In another bowl, combine oil, and egg. Add wet ingredients to dry and stir gently to combine. Add enough milk to moisten ingredients, up to 1/2 cup, stirring to combine.

Don't over mix.

6. If needed, add a little more milk, a tablespoon at a time, until mixture is moist but not wet or soupy.

7. Carefully remove hot skillet from oven and pour cornbread mixture into skillet. It will sizzle a bit.

8. Return pan to oven and bake 20-25 minutes or until golden brown and crisp.

Extra Extra!

If you want to try a truly traditional Southern cornbread, use stone ground cornmeal in place of the store-bought yellow or white cornmeal. Stone ground cornmeal is hard to find, even in Southern grocery stores now, but you can easily get it on the internet.

!51

Triple Chocolate Brownie Skillet Pie

This skillet pie takes brownies to a whole new level! Rich cocoa pairs with chocolate chips for a melty, ooey-gooey treat that will satisfy even the most discerning chocolate lover. Serves 6.

Ingredients:

- 2 eggs
- 1/2 C. Chocolate Chips
- 1 C. Sugar
- 1/2 C. Chopped nuts (I like pecans, but
- 1/2 C. melted butter or margarine, cooled

walnuts or even roasted peanuts are also

slightly

good!)

- 1/2 C. All Purpose Flour
- 1 teaspoon vanilla
- 1/8 teaspoon salt
- Crisco
- 1/3 C. Cocoa

!52

Instructions:

1. Preheat oven to 350 degrees.

2. Grease an 8" cast iron skillet lightly with Crisco and set aside.

3. Beat together eggs, melted butter and sugar.

4. In a separate bowl, stir together flour, cocoa and salt, then add to egg mixture. Add vanilla.

5. Beat until well blended.

6. Fold in chocolate chips and nuts.

7. Pour into prepared skillet and bake 30-35 minutes or until set at edges. (Pie will not test done in center.)

8. Cool and cut into wedges. Serve alone or with ice cream and a drizzle of chocolate syrup.

Peanut Butter Brownie Skillet Pie

Substitute peanut butter chips for the chocolate chips and chopped roasted peanuts for the pecans. Omit salt. Proceed as instructed. Serve with whipped cream.

!53

Cast Iron Buttermilk Brunch Cake

This surprisingly light coffee cake gets a delicious tang from Bavarian-style buttermilk, which has a thick texture—almost like sour cream. It pairs well with the sweetness of the brown sugar and crunch of pecans. Serves 8-10.

Ingredients:

- 1 18.25 package yellow cake mix (without

- 1/2 cup brown sugar

pudding)

- 2 teaspoons cinnamon

- 1 cup Bavarian-style buttermilk (not low-

- 1/4 c. chopped nuts

fat)

- shortening

- 1 stick butter, melted and slightly cooled

- Creamy Buttermilk Glaze (recipe follows)

- 5 eggs

!54

1. Preheat oven to 350 degrees.

2. Lightly grease a 12" cast iron skillet and set aside.

3. In a separate bowl, stir together the brown sugar, cinnamon and nuts. Set aside.

4. Using an electric mixer, beat first 3 ingredients together at medium speed until completely blended. Mixture will be thick, about the consistency of cookie dough.

5. Add eggs, 1 at a time until each is well incorporated. Pour about 2/3 of the batter into the skillet.

6. Sprinkle brown sugar mixture evenly over cake mixture, then pour remaining batter evenly over top.

7. Bake for 30-35 minutes, or until wooden pick inserted in center comes out clean.

8. Remove cake from oven and allow to cool for about 10 minutes.

9. Top with glaze, if desired. Serve warm right from the skillet.

Creamy Buttermilk Glaze

- 1/4 cup Bavarian-style buttermilk

- 2 tablespoons melted butter or margarine

- 1 1/2 cups powdered sugar, sifted

- 1/2 teaspoon vanilla

1. Stir buttermilk, powdered sugar and melted butter together until smooth and creamy.

Add vanilla extract and stir to combine. Pour over warm cake before serving.

2. If you can't find Bavarian-style buttermilk, substitute 3/4 cup regular buttermilk and 1/4 cup sour cream. Proceed as directed.

3. Do not use low-fat buttermilk or low-fat sour cream in this recipe.

!55

Part 2

Introduction

Cooking is an art. No doubt, almost everybody can cook but the magical taste which treats your taste buds comes only in the dishes prepared by dedicated or expert chefs. For instance, you always like to go to a restaurant when you feel like treating yourself. But it can be a little costly. So, what if you could get the same delicious and magical taste at your own home? What if you could cook like a chef? Is it possible? Yes, it definitely is. You just need to know the right tricks, ingredients and recipes, and who knows may be you will become the next master chef? To help you put the first step forward, a collection of 21 delicious vegetarian recipes has been incorporated in this book. Go ahead and evoke the chef in you.

Chapter 1: Delicious Vegetarian Recipes

Orzo Salad Topped With Buttermilk Dressing

Ingredients-

- Uncooked orzo- 1 cup
- Thawed and drained frozen whole kernel corn- 1 cup
- Quartered cherry tomatoes- 12
- Sliced green onions
- Rinsed and drained black beans- 1 can (~15 ounce)
- Low fat buttermilk- ¼ cup
- Chopped cilantro- 3 tbs
- Fresh lime juice- 2 tbs
- Light sour cream- 2 tbs
- Canola mayonnaise- 2 tbs
- Chili powder- 1 tsp
- Kosher salt- ½ tsp
- Black pepper- ¼ tsp
- Ground red pepper- ¼ tsp
- Crushed garlic cloves- 2
- Peeled and cut avocados- 1 (cut the avocado into 8 wedges)
- Chopped fresh parsley- 1 tbs

Directions-

1. Cook orzo as per directions given on its packet, but without any fats or salt.
2. Rinse and drain them well.
3. Put orzo, tomatoes, corn, onions and beans in a bowl and mix them.
4. Add some buttermilk, 2 tbs cilantro and all other ingredients in a separate bowl and whisk them together.
5. Drizzle this mixture over the orzo mixture and then mix well by tossing.
6. Top the final mixture with avocados.
7. Garnish it with parsley and the remaining 1 tbs of cilantro.

Broccoli- Ham Pasta Salad

Ingredients-

SALAD:

- Cooked pasta- 3 cups
- Chopped broccoli- 4 cups
- Diced ham- 1 and a ½ cups
- Diced bell pepper (red/ yellow)- ¼ cup
- Dices red onion- 1/3 cup
- Slices of 1 onion for garnishing
- Raisins- 1/3 cup
- Spinach leaves- 4 cups
- Radicchio leaves- 1 cup
- Ground pepper

CREAMY HERBED DRESSING-

1. Low fat mayonnaise- ½ cup

2. Non-fat plain yogurt- 1/3 cup
3. Reduced fat sour cream- ¼ cup
4. Vinegar (rice or white wine)- 3 tbs
5. Dijon mustard- 1tbs
6. Honey- 1tbs
7. Dried minced onion- 1 and a ½ tsp
8. Dried dill or tarragon- 1 ¼ tsp
9. Onion salt- ¼ tsp
10. Celery salt- ¼ tsp
11. White pepper

Directions-

1. For salad- Put all the ingredients; pasta, ham, broccoli, diced onion, raisins and bell pepper in a bowl and toss to mix them together.
2. For dressing- Put yogurt, mayonnaise, vinegar, sour cream, honey, mustard, tarragon or dill, onion, celery salt and onion salt in a bowl and blend them all together. Season this mixture with white pepper.
3. Add the dressing on top of the salad and toss them until they become well incorporated.
4. Cover the mixture and keep it in the refrigerator for about 30 minutes to 48 hours. This will help in blending all the flavors together.
5. Place the refrigerated mixture on a bed of radicchio and spinach and finally, garnish it with red onion slices.

Spinach- Chickpea Squash

Ingredients-

- Frozen gnocchi- 1 pound
- Extra virgin olive oil- 1 tbs and 1 tsp
- Sliced unpeeled 'delicata squash' or peeled 'butternut squash'- 2 cups (Slices should be thin and 1 to 2 inch long)
- Sliced shallots- ½ cup
- Minced garlic cloves- 2
- Vegetable broth- 1 can of 14 ounce
- Currants- 2tbs
- Chopped fresh age- 1tbs (1 tsp id dried and rubbed)
- Fresh ground pepper- ¼ tsp
- Coarsely chopped fresh spinach- 8 cups
- Rinsed chickpeas- 1 can of 15 ounce
- Balsamic vinegar- 2tbs

Directions-

1. Cook frozen gnocchi in boiling water as per the directions given on its packet.
2. Rinse, drain and dry the cooked gnocchi. (You can also shelf stable gnocchi instead of fresh gnocchi, but in that case just skip the first step)
3. Put 1 tbs oil in a non-stick skillet and heat it over medium flame.
4. Add gnocchi to the pan and cook with constant stirring until it starts to turn brown. It will take approximately 5 to 7 minutes.
5. Transfer the cooked gnocchi to a bowl.
6. Put 1 tsp oil, garlic, shallots and squash to the pan and cook for about 2 minutes with constant stirring.
7. Add broth, sage, pepper, and currants. Stir to mix them with other ingredients and bring them to boil.

8. Reduce the flame to simmer and then cook the squash for almost 6 – 8 minutes while stirring constantly.
9. Add gnocchi, chickpeas and spinach to the mixture and cook them together until the spinach becomes wilted. Keep stirring gently.
10. Drizzle some balsamic vinegar on top of the mixture.

Vegetarian Bibimbap

Ingredients-

- Sesame oil- 2 tbs
- Carrot matchsticks- 1 cup
- Zucchini matchsticks- 1 cup
- Drained bean sprouts- ½ can of about 14 ounce
- Drained canned bamboo shoots- 6 ounces
- Drained sliced mushrooms- 1 can of about 2.5 ounces
- Cooked rice- 2 cups (cooled)
- Sliced green onions- 1/3 cup
- Soy sauce- 2 tbs
- Ground black pepper- ¼ tsp
- Butter- 1 tbs
- Eggs- 3
- Salt

Directions-

1. Put sesame oil in a large skillet and heat it over a medium flame.
2. Cook zucchini and carrot in hot oil with constant stirring for about 5 minutes, until they become soft.
3. Add mushrooms, bean sprouts and bamboo, and stir well.

4. Cook for about next 5 to 6 minutes until the carrots become tender.
5. Add some salt and set the mixture aside in a bowl.
6. Put green onions, rice, black pepper and soy sauce in the same skillet and cook them until rice becomes hot. Keep stirring gently.
7. Melt some butter in a separate skillet over a medium flame and then fry each egg for about 3 minutes.
8. Turn the eggs once until the egg whites become firm but the yolks are runny still.
9. Divide the rice mixture into 3 separate bowls.
10. Top each rice mixture filled bowl with equally divided vegetable mixture and fried eggs.

Vegetarian Korma

Ingredients-

- Vegetable oil- 1 and a ½ tbs
- Diced small onion- 1
- Minced fresh ginger root- 1 tsp
- Minced garlic cloves- 4
- Cubed potatoes- 2
- Cubed carrots- 4
- Sliced and seeded fresh jalapeno pepper- 1
- Unsalted ground cashews- 3 tbs
- Tomato sauce- 1 can (~ 4 ounce)
- Curry powder- 1 and a ½ tbs
- Salt- 2 tsp
- Frozen green peas- 1 cup
- Chopped green bell pepper- ½

- Chopped red bell pepper- ½
- Heavy cream- 1 cup
- Fresh cilantro- 1 bunch

Directions-

1. Put the vegetable oil in a large skillet and heat it over a medium flame.
2. Add onions to it and cook them until they become tender.
3. Add garlic and ginger, and then after about 1 minute, add carrots, potatoes, cashews, tomato sauce, jalapenos, curry powder and salt.
4. Cook the ingredients while constantly stirring them until potatoes become tender enough. This process would take up to 10 minutes.
5. Add red bell pepper, green bell pepper, cream and peas to the skillet and stir well.
6. Reduce the heat to simmer and cover the skillet for next 10 minutes.
7. Garnish the mixture with finely chopped cilantro.

Creamy Barley Salad With Apples

Ingredients-

- Pearl barley- ½ cup
- Plain- Low fat yogurt- ½ cup
- Extra virgin olive oil- 2 tbs
- Fresh lemon juice- 2 tbs
- Dijon mustard- 1 tsp
- Sliced celery- 2 stalks
- Thinly sliced apple- 1

- Chopped fresh mint- ¼ cup
- Arugula- 2 bunches (remove thick stems)
- Black pepper
- Salt

Directions-

1. Add 1 and ½ cups of water, ½ tsp salt and the barley in a medium sized sauce pan and bring them to boil.
2. Reduce the flame to medium and cover the saucepan.
3. Simmer it for about next 25 – 3- minutes until the barley absorbs all the water and becomes tender.
4. Drain the pan if there is any water left and spread the barley on a rimmed baking sheet.
5. Add yogurt, lemon juice, oil, mustard, ¼ tsp pepper and ½ tsp salt in a bowl and whisk them together.
6. Add cooled barley, apple, celery and mint to the whisked mixture and toss them to mix well.
7. Place equally divided arugula in two or three bowls and top it with the freshly prepared barley mixture.

Broccoli Meatballs With Garlic And Tomato Sauce

Ingredients-

MEATBALLS-
- Broccoli florets- 4 cups
- Raw almonds- 1 cup
- Grated Parmesan cheese- ¼ cup
- Fresh Basil, finely chopped- ¼ cup
- Fresh parsley, finely chopped- ¼ cup

- Minced garlic cloves- 2
- Cayenne pepper- 1/8 tsp
- Eggs- 2

GARLIC AND TOMATO SAUCE-
1. Olive oil- 1 tbs
2. Diced white onion- ¼ cup
3. Finely chopped garlic cloves- 1
4. Crushed tomatoes- 1 can of about 28 ounce

Directions-

For meatballs-

1. Preheat the oven to about 350' F.
2. Using a parchment paper, line the baking sheet.
3. Steam the broccoli florets for approximately 10 minutes, until they become bright green in color and tender.
4. Put it aside to cool.
5. Put raw almond in the blender and process to finely ground them.
6. Transfer the grounded almonds to a large bowl.
7. Put the steamed broccoli in the blender and process it well until finely chopped.
8. Transfer it to the bowl containing almonds.
9. Add basil, parmesan, garlic, cayenne, parsley, pepper and salt to the mixture of broccoli and almonds and mix them together.
10. Whisk 2 eggs in a separate bowl and then add it to the broccoli mixture.
11. Stir well.
12. Mould the mixture into the shape of small meatballs.

13. Place these meatballs on the baking sheet and bake them for approximately 25 minutes, until they turn golden- brown.

For garlic and tomato sauce-

1. Put the olive oil in a large sized sauce pan and heat it over medium flame.
2. Add garlic and onion. Then, cook for next 5 minutes, until onion becomes tender and soft.
3. Add crushed tomatoes to the pan and cook for next 20 minutes, while stirring gently and occasionally, till the sauce becomes thick.
4. Sprinkle some pepper and salt.

Tomatillo Pizza-Dillas

Ingredients-

- Rinsed, husked, sliced tomatillos- 4
- Olive oil- ½ tsp
- Dried oregano- ½ tsp
- Reduced fat provolone cheese- 8 slices
- Corn tortillas- 16 (5 inch)
- Prepared salsa- ½ cup
- Reduced fat jalapeno- jack cheese, grated- 1 cup (~ 4 ounce)

Directions-

1. Preheat the oven to about 425' F.
2. Put the tomatillos, dried oregano and olive in a medium sized bowl and toss to mix.

3. Sprinkle some pepper and salt over the mixture and set it aside.
4. Put 1 slice of provolone cheese between 2 tortillas and place over the baking sheet.
5. Repeat the step for all tortillas.
6. Top the crusts of each tortilla with 1 tbs salsa.
7. Drain the tortilla slices of any excess water.
8. Arrange these slices on top of the pizzas.
9. Sprinkle some grated Jack cheese over it.
10. Bake each of them for approximately 6 to 8 minutes until the cheese melts and the tortillas become soft.
11. Cool it down for about 3 to 4 minutes.

Vegetable Meat Loaf

Ingredients-

For meat loaf-

- Red bell pepper- 1
- Green bell pepper- 1
- Coarsely chopped Cremini mushrooms- 2 pounds
- Olive oil- 1 tbs
- Asparagus pieces- 1 cup (1/2 inch)
- Chopped red onion- ½ cup
- Japanese bread crumbs/ Panko- 1 cup
- Chopped and toasted walnuts- 1 cup
- Chopped- fresh bail- 2 tbs
- Ketchup- 1 tbs
- Dijon mustard- 1 tsp
- Kosher salt- ½ tsp
- Freshly ground- black pepper- ½ tsp

- Lightly beaten eggs- 2
- Cooking spray

For topping-

1. Ketchup- 2 tbs
2. Vegetable broth or vodka- 1 tbs
3. Dijon mustard- ½ tsp

Directions-

Preheat the boiler on high.

Meatloaf preparation-

1. Cut the bell pepper into 2 halves vertically and discard the membranes and the seeds.
2. Place them on a baking sheet lined with parchment paper with the skin side facing upwards and flatten them with hand.
3. Broil for approximately 12 minutes until it starts turning black.
4. Place them in a paper bag and fold it tightly.
5. Let it stand alone for about 10 minutes.
6. Peel and then chop them finely.
7. Put the bell peppers in a large sized bowl.
8. Reduce the temperature of the oven to about 350' F.
9. Put 1/4th mushrooms in the food processor and blend them well until they are finely chopped.
10. Transfer the mushrooms in a separate bowl.
11. Repeat the same procedure thrice with the rest of the mushrooms.

12. Take a large sized non-stick skillet and heat it over medium-high flame.
13. Add olive oil to the pan and swirl it to coat the whole surface.
14. Put the finely chopped mushrooms to the pan and sauté them for next 15 minutes while stirring continuously.
15. Add the mushrooms to the bowl of bell peppers.
16. Wipe the pan with a clean paper towel.
17. Put onion and asparagus in the pan and sauté them for next 6 minutes while stirring constantly until they become soft.
18. Add this onion mixture to the mushroom-bell pepper mixture.
19. Place the breadcrumbs evenly on the parchment lined baking sheet.
20. Bake the breadcrumbs at 350' F, until they start turning gold for next 10 minutes.
21. Add the remaining ingredients and the breadcrumbs to the mushroom mixture and stir well.
22. Coat a 9 by 5 inch loaf pan with cooking spray and spoon the mushroom mixture into it.
23. Gently, press the mixture to pack.
24. Bake it at a temperature of 350' F for approximately 45 minutes.

Topping Preparation-

1. Add 2 tbs ketchup and the topping ingredients in a bowl and mix well.
2. Coat the meat loafs with this ketchup mixture.
3. Bake the brushed/ coated meat loafs for 10 more minutes.
4. Let them stand aside for further 10 minutes and then cut into slices.

Veggistrone

Ingredients-

- Extra virgin olive oil- 2 tbs
- Chopped onions- 1 cups
- Chopped celery- 2 cups
- Chopped- green bell pepper- 1 cup
- Minced garlic cloves- 4
- Chopped cabbage- 3 cups
- Chopped cauliflower- 3 cups
- Chopped carrots- 2 cups
- Thawed frozen Green beans- 2 cups
- Vegetable broth (low sodium)- 8 cups
- Water- 2 cups
- Tomato sauce- 1 can (15 ounce)
- Diced tomatoes- 1 can (14 ounce)
- Rinsed kidney beans- 1 can (15 ounce)
- Bay leaf- 1
- Thawed, frozen chopped spinach- 1 can (10 ounce)
- Fresh basil, thinly sliced- ½ cup
- Parmesan cheese, freshly grated- 10 tbs

Directions-

1. Put some oil in a large soup-pot and heat it over medium flame.
2. Add garlic, onion, bell pepper and celery to the pan and cook for about 13 – 15 minutes while constantly stirring until they become soft.

3. Add carrots, green beans cauliflower and cabbage, and cook for next 10 minutes while occasionally stirring.
4. Add water, vegetable broth, tomatoes, tomato sauce, bay leaf and beans to the pan.
5. Cover the pan and bring it to boil.
6. Reduce the flame to simmer and cook for about next 20 – 25 minutes, pan covered only partially until the vegetables become soft.
7. Add spinach, stir it well and simmer for further 10 minutes.
8. Discard the bay-leaf.
9. Add basil and stir well.
10. Top it with 1 tbs cheese.

Creamy Avocado And White Bean Wrap

Ingredients-

- Cider vinegar- 2 tbs
- Canola oil- 1 tbs
- Finely chopped 'chiptole chile (smoked jalapenos)' in 'adobo sauce (a flavorful sauce)'
- Salt- ¼ tsp
- Shredded red cabbage- 2 cups
- Shredded carrot- 1
- Fresh chopped cilantro- ¼ cup
- Rinsed white beans- 1 can (15 ounce)
- Ripe avocado- 1
- Sharp- cheddar cheese, shredded- ½ cup
- Minced red onions- 2 tbs
- Tortillas/ whole wheat wraps- 4 (~8 – 10 inch)

Directions-

1. Put vinegar oil, salt, oil, chipotle chile in a medium sized bowl and whisk them together.
2. Add carrot, cilantro and cabbage to the whisked mixture and toss it to combine all the ingredients.
3. Mash the avocado and the beans in a separate medium sized bowl using a fork.
4. Add onion and chess. Stir well.
5. Place the wraps/ tortillas on a flat surface and then spread approximately around ½ cup bean avocado mixture onto it.
6. Top it with 2/3 cup carrot cabbage slaw and roll the wrap.
7. Repeat the same step with the remaining wraps and mixtures.

Ravioli And Vegetable Pasta Soup

Ingredients-

- Extra virgin olive oil- 1 tbs
- Diced, thawed- frozen onion and bell pepper mix- 2 cups
- Minced garlic cloves- 2
- Crushed red pepper- ¼ tsp
- Fire roasted, crushed tomatoes- 1 can (28 ounce)
- Vegetable broth- 1 can (15 ounce)
- Hot water- 1 and a ½ cup
- Marjoram or Dried basil- 1 tsp
- Whole wheat fresh/ frozen cheese ravioli- 1 can (6 – 9 ounce)
- Freshly ground pepper

Directions-

1. Put some oil in a large sauce-pan and heat it over medium flame.
2. Add garlic, crushed pepper and onion-pepper mix to the pan and cook for a minute while stirring.
3. Add basil, water, tomatoes and vegetable broth and bring them to boil.
4. Add ravioli to the pan and then cook for 3 minutes lesser than the time given on the packet.
5. Add zucchini and again bring the mixture to boil.
6. Cook for approximately 3 minutes until zucchini becomes crispy and tender.
7. Sprinkle some pepper over it.

Pearl Barley, Parsnip And Sage Rositto

Ingredients-

- Butter- 25 g
- Finely chopped onion- 1
- Peeled and cut into 'chunks'- Parsnip- 4
- Crushed garlic clove- 1
- Shredded sage leaves- 10
- Rinsed pearl barley- 400 g
- Hot vegetable stock- 1.4 liter
- Grated Parmesan- 25 g

Directions-

1. Put 25 g butter in a large sauce-pan and heat it over medium flame.
2. Add onion and salt to the pan and cook for about 5 minutes.

3. Add parsnips to the pan and turn up the heat. Cook for about next 8 – 10 minutes, while stirring occasionally, until the parsnips start turning brown.
4. Add sage and garlic to the pan and mix well.
5. Add barley and then stir to coat and mix well.
6. Pour the vegetable stock and bring it to boil.
7. Turn the heat down to simmer and then, cook for next 35 to 40 minutes, until the pearl barley becomes tender and all the water is absorbed.
8. Turn off the flame and top the mixture with butter and parmesan. Let them melt.
9. Stir the mixture (rositto) well.
10. Place it in a dish and top with some black pepper, some more sage and parmesan.

Porridge With Blueberry Compote

Ingredients-

- Porridge oats- 6 tbs
- Fat free Greek style yogurt- ½ tub (200 ml)
- Frozen blueberries- ½ pack (350 g)
- Honey- 1 tsp (optional)

Directions-

1. Cook the oats with water in a non-stick pan. Stir continuously for about 2 minutes, until it thickens.
2. Remove the oats from the flame and add 1/3 rd yogurt to it.
3. Put the frozen blueberries, honey (optional) and 1 tbs water in a separate pan and then gently poach them until they

become tender and thawed. (The shape of blueberries should remain same)
4. Put the porridge into serving bowls and top with remaining yogurt.
5. Spoon over the porridge- yogurt mixture with blueberries.

Italian Vegetable Hoagies

Ingredients-

- Thinly sliced, separated into 'rings'-red onion- ¼ cup
- Rinsed, coarsely chopped artichoke hearts- 1 can (14 ounce)
- Diced and seeded tomato- 1
- Balsamic vinegar- 2 tbs
- Dried oregano- 1 tsp
- Extra virgin olive oil- 1 tbs
- Whole grain long baguette- 1 (16 – 20 inch long)
- Provolone cheese- 2 slices
- Shredded romaine lettuce- 2 cups
- Sliced pepperoncini- ¼ cup (optional)

Directions-

1. Put onion rings in a small sized bowl.
2. Add cold water to it and cover the bowl.
3. Set it aside.
4. Add tomato, artichoke hearts, oregano, vinegar and oil in a medium sized bowl and mix well.
5. Cut the baguette into 4 equal pieces.
6. Split all the 4 pieces horizontally.
7. Pull out approximately half the soft bread from each side.
8. Drain the onions. Pat them dry.

9. Divide the provolone among bottom pieces of the whole grain baguette.
10. Spread the artichoke mixture and then top it with lettuce, pepperoncini and onion.
11. Cover the whole grain baguette tops.

Spicy Root And Lentil Casserole

Ingredients-

- Vegetable oil- 2 tbs
- Chopped onion- 1
- Crushed garlic cloves- 2
- Peeled, cut into 'chunks' potatoes- 700 g
- Thickly sliced carrots- 4
- Curry powder- 2 tbs
- Vegetable stock- 1 liter
- Red lentils- 100 g
- Roughly chopped fresh coriander- 1 small bunch
- Naan bread
- Low fat Yogurt

Directions-

1. Put vegetable oil in a pan and heat it over a medium flame.
2. Add garlic and onion and cook for next 3 minutes with occasional stirring for next 3 to 4 minutes.
3. Add parsnips, carrots and potatoes, and then, turn the heat up.
4. Cook for about 6 to 7 minutes with constant stirring, until all the vegetable start turning golden.
5. Add curry powder and stir well.

6. Pour in the vegetable stock and bring the mixture to boil.
7. Reduce the flame to simmer, add the lentils and then cover the pan.
8. Cook for approximately 15 to 20 minutes until the sauce becomes thick and the vegetable and lentils become soft and tender.
9. Season with 2/3 rd of the coriander, heat for about a minute or two while stirring constantly.
10. Top it with the remaining coriander and yogurt.
11. Heat the naan bread and serve together.

Khoya Stuffed Matar Ki Tikki

Ingredients-

For Tikki-

- Black cumin- 1 and a ½ tsp
- Asafetida- 1 pinch, mixed with water
- Desi ghee/ vegetable oil- 1 and a ½ tbs
- Chopped green chillies- 3 tsp
- Chopped ginger- 2 tbs
- Peas- 1 bowl
- Turneric powder- ¼ tsp
- Coriander powder- 1 tsp
- Gram flour- 2 to 3 tbs
- Salt

For Filling-

1. Khoya/ thickened milk- 60 to 70 g
2. Chopped green chillies- 2 tsp

3. Chopped pistachio- 3 tsp
4. Chopped coriander leaves- 1 tsp
5. Chopped dates- 2 to 3

Directions-

1. Add ghee/ vegetable oil, cumin, asafetida water, ginger and green chillies in a separate pan and sauté for about 30 seconds.
2. Add turmeric powder, salt, coriander powder and peas and sauté them until the peas start turning brownish.
3. Blend the cooked peas in the food processor, to make a fine paste.
4. Add some gram flour in order to make a tiff- mixture.
5. Crumble the khoya in a large bowl.
6. Add dates, coriander leaves, pistachio, chillies and mix well.
7. Stuff the stiffened pea mixture with the khoya filling.
8. Heat some oil a large pan and then shallow fry or grill these tikkis.

Vegetarian Biryani

Ingredients-

- Rinsed rice- 1 and ½ cup
- Water- 5 cups
- Salt
- Ghee/ butter- 1 tbs
- Cooking oil- 1 tbs
- Chopped onion- 1
- Minced garlic cloves- 2
- Fresh ginger, grated- 1 tbs

- Ground cumin- ½ tsp
- Turmeric powder- 1 tsp
- Curry powder- ½ tsp
- Cayenne powder- 1/8 tsp
- Peeled and cut into 1 and a ½ inch chunks- potato- 1
- Chopped Carrots- 2
- Frozen peas- 1 can (10 ounce)
- Plain yogurt- ¼ cup
- Minced jalapeno chile, ribs and seeds removed- 1
- Tomato- 1
- Cilantro leaf- ½ cup

Directions-

1. Pour 3 cups water in a large container. Add a pinch of salt and bring it to boil.
2. Put in the rice, stir well and then boil again for about 10 to 15 minutes until the rice absorb all the water.
3. Drain the rice, if required, and then, cover the container, to keep rice warm.
4. Melt the butter with vegetable oil in a large frying pan over the moderately low flame.
5. Add onion to the pan and cook for about 5 minutes until they become soft and translucent.
6. Add ginger and garlic, stir and cook for next 1 minute.
7. Add cumin, curry powder, cayenne and turmeric powder, stir and cook for further 1 minute.
8. Add the carrots, potato, peas, salt and the remaining 2 cups of water to the pan.
9. Turn the heat up to simmer the vegetables for about 10 minutes until there is no water remaining in the pan and the vegetables become tender.

10. Stir in the rice and yogurt and top with tomato, cilantro and jalapeno.

Marinated Aubergine And Rocket Salad

Ingredients-

- Abergines- cut into 'chunks'- 2
- Olive oil- 3 tbs
- Balsamic vinegar- 2 tbs
- Sultanas- Handful
- Rocket- 50 g

Directions-

1. Preheat the oven to 400' F.
2. Put the aubergines in a large roasting tin, top with some seasoning and 2 tbs olive oil and toss to mix well.
3. Toast the aubergines for approximately 30 minutes until they become soft and golden in color.
4. Add balsamic vinegar, remaining oil and sultanas and toss the mixture.
5. Place the rocket in a serving dish and scatter the cooked aubergines over it.

Ingredients-

- Abergines- cut into 'chunks'- 2
- Olive oil- 3 tbs
- Balsamic vinegar- 2 tbs
- Sultanas- Handful
- Rocket- 50 g

Directions-

1. Preheat the oven to 400' F.
2. Put the aubergines in a large roasting tin, top with some seasoning and 2 tbs olive oil and toss to mix well.
3. Toast the aubergines for approximately 30 minutes until they become soft and golden in color.
4. Add balsamic vinegar, remaining oil and sultanas and toss the mixture.
5. Place the rocket in a serving dish and scatter the cooked aubergines over it.

Tofu Rancheros

Ingredients-

- Olive oil- 1 and a ½ tbs
- Sliced onion- 1 and a ½ cup
- Green bell pepper, cut into thin strips- 1 and a ½ cup
- Drained, dried, cut into 6 slabs- firm/ soft tofu- 1 can (16 ounce)
- Mild salsa- 1 cup
- Diced tomatoes- 1 cup
- Minced and seeded fresh jalapeno chiles- 2
- Nutritional yeast- 2 tbs (optional)
- Ground cumin- 1 tsp
- Ground turmeric- ¼ tsp (optional)
- Chopped cilantro leaves- 1 cup
- Warmed corn tortillas- 8

Directions-

1. Put oil in a large skillet and heat over a medium flame.
2. Add onion and sauté for about 5 minutes.
3. Add bell pepper to the skillet and sauté for next 5 minutes until they start turning brown.
4. Add tofu, crumbling every slice.
5. Add tomatoes, jalapeno chiles, salsa, yeast, turmeric and cumin. Cook for about 5 to 8 minutes.
6. Add cilantro, stir well and then season with pepper and salt.
7. Divide the mixture equally among the tortillas.
8. Serve with salsa.

Fontal Polenta With Mushroom Sauté

Ingredients-

- Olive oil- 2 tbs
- Chopped exotic mushroom blend- 2 packs (4 ounce)
- Pre-sliced cremini mushrooms- 1 pack (8 ounce)
- Minced fresh thyme- 1 tsp
- Minced fresh oregano- ½ tsp
- Chopped garlic cloves- 3
- Vegetable broth- 1 and a 1/2 cup + 1/3 cup
- Fresh lemon juice- 2 tsp
- Salt- 1 tsp
- Black pepper- 1/8 tsp
- 2% Reduced fat milk- 2 cups
- Instant Polenta- ¾ cup
- Shredded fontal cheese- 1 cup (4 ounce)

Directions-

1. Put oil in a skillet and heat over medium flame.

2. Add mushrooms to the skillet and sauté for about 4 minutes.
3. Add garlic and sauté for next 1 minute.
4. Add lemon juice, 1/3 cup vegetable broth, pepper and salt to the skillet and stir well.
5. Pour milk and 1 and a ½ cup vegetable broth in a separate pan and bring them to boil.
6. Put in Polenta and stir constantly for the next 4 minutes.
7. Put in half of the cheese and salt. Stir well.
8. Divide the Polenta among 4 serving dishes.
9. Top it with the remaining cheese.
10. Broil for about 5 minutes.
11. Top with ½ cup mushrooms.

Cast Iron Fudge Brownies

Ingredients

1 ¼ cups sugar

3 large eggs

1 cup all-purpose flour (spooned and leveled)

¼ cup Dutch-processed cocoa powder (spooned and leveled)

½ teaspoon salt

4 tablespoons unsalted butter

¼ cup heavy cream

8 ounces bittersweet chocolate, coarsely chopped

Directions

Preheat oven to 350 degrees.

In a large bowl, whisk together sugar and eggs. In another bowl, whisk together flour, cocoa, and salt.

In a medium ovenproof nonstick skillet, bring butter and cream to a simmer over medium. Add chocolate; reduce to medium-low. Cook, stirring constantly, until chocolate has melted, about 1 minute. Remove from heat, and let cool 5 minutes.

Add chocolate mixture to sugar mixture, whisking until blended (reserve skillet)

Fold in flour mixture. Pour batter into skillet.

Bake until a toothpick inserted in center comes out clean, about 40 minutes.

Serve from skillet, warm or at room temperature.

Apple Cobbler

Ingredients

6.75 ounces all-purpose flour (about 1 1/2 cups), divided

12 cups thinly sliced peeled Fuji apple (about 4 pounds)

2/3 cup sugar, divided

2 tablespoons butter, melted

2 teaspoons vanilla extract

3/4 teaspoon salt, divided

1/2 teaspoon ground cinnamon

1/4 teaspoon ground nutmeg

1/2 cup water

2 teaspoons baking powder

1/4 cup chilled butter, cut into small pieces

1 cup low-fat buttermilk

Directions

Preheat oven to 375F°.

Weigh or lightly spoon flour into dry measuring cups; level with a knife. Combine 25 ounces (about 1/2 cup) flour, apple, 1/3 cup sugar, 2 tablespoons butter, vanilla, 1/2 teaspoon salt, cinnamon, and nutmeg in a large bowl, tossing well.

Spoon into a large cast-iron Dutch oven. Add 1/2 cup water.

Combine remaining 5 ounces (about 1 cup) flour, remaining 1/3 cup sugar, remaining 1/4 teaspoon salt, and baking powder in a medium bowl; cut in 1/4 cup butter with a pastry blender or 2 knives until mixture resembles coarse meal.

Add buttermilk; stir until just moist. Drop batter by tablespoonfuls over apple mixture. Bake at 375° for 1 hour or until bubbly and browned. Serve warm.

Apple Brownie

Ingredients

1 cup all-purpose flour

1/2 cup white sugar

1/2 cup brown sugar

1/4 teaspoon salt

2 teaspoons ground cinnamon

1 teaspoon ground nutmeg

1/2 teaspoon ground cloves

2 eggs, lightly beaten

1 teaspoon vanilla extract

1/2 cup melted butter

2 cups apples - peeled, cored and chopped

1/2 cup chopped pecans

1 tablespoon butter

Directions

Preheat an oven to 350 degrees F (175 degrees C). Place an 8- or 9-inch cast iron skillet into the oven to preheat. Whisk together the flour, white sugar, brown sugar, salt, cinnamon, nutmeg, and cloves in a bowl; set aside.

Beat together the eggs, vanilla extract, and melted butter in a mixing bowl. Toss the apples and pecans in the flour mixture, then stir into the egg mixture until combined. Melt 1 tablespoon of butter in the preheated skillet, swirling to coat the pan.

Pour the batter into the hot pan, and replace into the oven. Bake until the sides are dry and a toothpick inserted into the center of the brownie comes out clean, about 40 minutes. Cool in the skillet 20 minutes before removing and slicing.

Skillet Pecan Pie

Ingredients

1/2 (14.1-oz.) package refrigerated piecrusts

1 tablespoon powdered sugar

4 large eggs

1 1/2 cups firmly packed light brown sugar

1/2 cup butter, melted and cooled to room temperature

1/2 cup granulated sugar

1/2 cup chopped pecans

2 tablespoons all-purpose flour

2 tablespoons milk

1 1/2 teaspoons bourbon

1 1/2 cups pecan halves

Directions

Preheat oven to 325°. Fit piecrust into a 10-inch cast-iron skillet; sprinkle piecrust with powdered sugar.

Whisk eggs in a large bowl until foamy; whisk in brown sugar and next 6 ingredients. Pour mixture into piecrust, and top with pecan halves.

Bake at 325F° for 30 minutes; reduce oven temperature to 300°, and bake 30 more minutes. Turn oven off, and let pie stand in oven, with door closed, 3 hours.

Cast Iron Vanilla Cake

Ingredients

1 1/2 cups flour

1 1/2 cups sugar

1 1/2 teaspoons baking powder

1 1/2 teaspoons vanilla

1 pinch salt

3 eggs

1 cup whipping cream

¼ cup butter

2 tablespoons sugar

2 teaspoons cinnamon

Directions

Preheat oven to 350F. Grease and flour a 9 or 10 inch iron skillet.

Mix 2 tbsp sugar and 2 tsp cinnamon together and set aside.

Put flour, 1 1/2 cup sugar, baking powder, vanilla, salt, eggs, and whipping cream together in large bowl. Beat with mixer till well blended.

Pour in prepared skillet and bake 35 to 45 minutes.

When done place on wire rack.

Spread top generously with the 1/2 stick of butter and sprinkle with sugar and cinnamon.

Chocolate Chip Skillet Cookie

Ingredients

¾ cup butter

½ cup sugar

¾ cup light brown sugar

2 cups flour

1 teaspoon baking soda

½ teaspoon salt

1 egg

2 teaspoons vanilla extract

1 ½ cups chocolate chips

¾ cup nuts (optional)

Directions

Cream butter and both sugars. Sift together the flour, baking soda, and salt. Set aside.

Add the egg and vanilla to the butter mixture. Add the flour mixture a little at a time.

Stir the chips and nuts in by hand.

Press into a 10 inch skillet and bake at 350F for 25 minutes.

Cast Iron Oatmeal Chocolate Cookie

Ingredients

1/2 cup butter

1/2 cup brown sugar

1/2 cup white sugar

1 teaspoon vanilla extract

2 eggs

1 cup all-purpose flour

1/2 teaspoon baking soda

1/4 teaspoon salt

1/2 cup old-fashioned oats

1 cup semi-sweet chocolate chunks or chips

1/4 cup salted caramel sauce

Directions

Preheat the oven to 350F.

Melt butter in a heated 8-inch cast iron skillet. Whisk in sugars and vanilla. Allow pan to cool about 5 minutes.

Carefully whisk eggs into the sugar mixture.

In a small bowl, combine the flour, baking soda, salt, and oats. Add the dry mixture to the skillet until just combined. Fold in chocolate chips. Drizzle 1/4 cup of the caramel over the dough.

Bake for 15-18 minutes, or until beginning to turn golden on top and around the edges but still soft in the center. Do not over bake. Remove from the oven and let cool for 5 minutes.

Drizzle with chocolate syrup and caramel syrup and lightly sprinkle with sea salt. Top with scoops of vanilla ice cream and serve immediately.

Chocolate Skillet Cookie

Ingredients

2 ounces semisweet chocolate

3 tablespoons canola oil

2 tablespoons unsalted butter

1/2 cup brown sugar

1/4 cup granulated sugar

1 large egg

3/4 cup all-purpose flour

1/2 cup unsweetened cocoa

1/2 teaspoon baking soda

1/2 teaspoon salt

2 1/2 ounces milk chocolate, chopped

Directions

Preheat oven to 350°. Combine semisweet chocolate, canola oil, and butter in a bowl. Microwave at HIGH 45 seconds, stirring occasionally.

Stir in brown sugar, granulated sugar, and egg. Stir in flour, cocoa, baking soda, and salt. Stir in chopped milk chocolate.

Scrape into a 10-inch cast-iron skillet. Bake at 350° for 19 minutes.

Apple Skillet Cake

Ingredients

3/4 cup flour

1 cup sugar, divided

1 teaspoon cinnamon

1 teaspoon baking powder

1/4 teaspoon ground cloves

1/4 teaspoon salt

3 medium baking apples, cored and sliced into 1/4 inch wedges

1 tablespoon lemon juice

1/3 cup bacon drippings

3/4 cup milk or 3/4 cup cold coffee

1 large egg, whisked

Directions

In a medium bowl mix 1/2 cup sugar, flour, cinnamon, baking powder, salt and cloves.

In another bowl, combine apples and lemon juice. Add remaining sugar.

Melt drippings in a 9-10" oven proof skillet.

Add egg and coffee or milk to flour mix and mix well.

Pour batter into skillet over the melted drippings - Do not mix it. Arrange the apple mix atop the batter.

Bake at 350F in the oven for 45 minutes until the batter is puffy and set and the apples are tender. Let cool for 20 minutes, then serve.

Fudge Skillet Cake

Ingredients

1 tablespoon vegetable shortening or 1 tablespoon butter

1 tablespoon all-purpose flour

18 $\frac{1}{4}$ ounces packaged cake mix

3 eggs (or as needed for cake mix)

$\frac{1}{3}$ cup oil (or as needed for cake mix)

1 $\frac{1}{3}$ cups water (or as needed for your cake mix)

4 ounces semi-sweet chocolate baking squares, coarsely chopped

12 ounces caramel ice cream topping, divided

$\frac{1}{2}$ cup pecans, chopped

Directions

Preheat oven to 350F degrees.

Grease and flour bottom and sides of skillet with shortening and flour, tap out excess flour.

Prepare cake mix according to package directions. Gently pour batter over bottom of skillet, spreading evenly.

Bake, uncovered, 30-35 minutes or until toothpick inserted in center comes out clean.

Carefully, remove skillet; cool cake. Loosen edges of cake and carefully invert onto platter.

Place chocolate and half of the icecream topping in microwave; cook on high 30-60 seconds or until chocolate is melted and mixture is smooth.

Spread caramel mixture over cake. Sprinkle pecans over cake.

Drizzle with remaining ice cream topping. Let stand until topping is set. Cut into wedges.

Serve with ice cream if desired.

Cast Iron Almond Peach Tart

Ingredients

1/3 cup sliced almonds

1 1/2 cups all-purpose flour

1 tablespoon granulated sugar

3/4 teaspoon salt

1/2 cup (1 stick) cold unsalted butter, cut into 8 pieces

3 to 4 tablespoons ice water

1/4 teaspoon almond extract

8 to 9 large peaches (about 2 3/4 pounds), pitted and sliced about 1/2 inch thick

3/4 cup granulated sugar

1 1/2 tablespoons cornstarch

1/4 teaspoon ground Saigon cinnamon

1 large egg

1 tablespoon water

1 tablespoon turbinado or granulated sugar for garnish

Directions

Toast the almonds: Preheat the oven to 300°. Scatter the almonds in a single layer on a baking sheet and bake, stirring occasionally, until golden brown, about 15 minutes. Remove from the oven and cool completely.

Make the pastry: Process the almonds in a blender or food processor until finely chopped. Add the flour, granulated sugar, and salt and pulse to combine. Add the butter and pulse until it resembles small peas.

Add the ice water, 1 tablespoon at a time, and almond extract, and process just until the dough comes together and forms a ball around the blades. Do not over rocess. Remove the dough from the processor, wrap it in plastic wrap, and chill at least 30 minutes or overnight.

Place a rack in the upper third of the oven and preheat to 375F°.

Make the filling: Place the peach slices in a large bowl. In a small bowl, stir together the granulated sugar, cornstarch, and cinnamon until well blended. Add the sugar mixture to the peaches, stirring gently.

Turn the dough out onto a floured pastry cloth or surface and roll into a 16-inch circle using a floured rolling pin.

Fold it in half, transfer to an ungreased 10-inch cast iron skillet, and gently unfold the pastry, fitting it into the bottom of the pan and allowing the excess pastry to hang over the edge.

Spoon the peach mixture into the pastry, mounding it in the middle. Gently fold the edges of the pastry up around the filling, overlapping them in soft folds. Take care that the pastry doesn't tear around the edge of the tart or the juices will escape during baking.

Whisk together the egg and water in a small bowl. Brush the egg wash over the pastry and sprinkle it with the turbinado sugar. Bake until the pastry is golden brown and the fruit is hot and bubbly, 35 to 40 minutes. Let cool for 1 hour to set the juices and serve warm

Apple Caramel Cake

Ingredients

2 $\frac{1}{3}$ cups flour

1 $\frac{1}{2}$ cups granulated sugar

2 teaspoons baking soda

½ teaspoon salt

1 teaspoon cinnamon

¼ teaspoon ground nutmeg

4 cups apples, peeled and grated (about 1 1/2 pounds)

½ cup vegetable shortening

2 eggs

Frosting

⅓ cup butter

½ cup light brown sugar

3 tablespoons whole milk

½ teaspoon vanilla extract

1 ½ cups powdered sugar

½ pecans, chopped (to garnish)

Directions

Preheat oven to 350F.

Butter a 10-inch cast iron skillet, dust with flour, and tap out excess.

To make the cake, combine the flour, sugar, baking soda, salt, cinnamon and nutmeg in a large bowl and mix well.

Add the apples, shortening and eggs to the flour mixture and beat with an electric mixer on medium speed until well blended. The batter will be stiff. Spread the batter evenly in the skillet.

Bake until a toothpick inserted in the center of the cake comes out clean, 40-45 minutes. Cool in the pan.

To make the frosting, melt the butter in a small saucepan over medium heat. Add the brown sugar and stir until the sugar dissolves. Add the milk and bring to a boil.

Pour into a mixing bowl and let cool for 10 minutes. Add the vanilla extract and powdered sugar and beat with a whisk until creamy or use an electric mixer.

The frosting will thicken as it cools. Spread evenly over the cooled apple cake. Sprinkle the chopped pecans over the top.

Cast Iron Pineapple Skillet Sponge Cake

Ingredients

2 tablespoons butter

$\frac{3}{4}$ cup brown sugar

7 pineapple slices

whole nutmeats

7 maraschino cherries

Batter

3 egg yolks

3 stiff-beaten egg whites

1 ½ cups sugar (divided)

½ cup boiling water

1 ½ cups cake flour

¼ teaspoon salt

1 teaspoon baking powder

Directions

Topping: In a heavy 8" ovenproof skillet (cast iron) melt butter and add brown sugar.

Arrange pineapple slices over mixture; place nut meats between slices and place a cherry in the center of each slice.

Pour following batter over.

Batter: Beat egg yolks until thick and lemon colored, add 1/2 cup of sugar, and continue beating.

Add water, then fold in remaining cup of sugar sifted with flour, salt, and baking powder.

Beat well and fold in egg whites.

Pour over pineapple in skillet and bake in a 325F 45 minutes.

Cool, run knife around edge to loosen, and turn out on a large platter, pineapple side up.

If desired, serve with whipped cream.

Peach Upside Down Cake

Ingredients

2 tablespoons butter

1 cup brown sugar

1 (29 ounce) can peach slices

¼ cup maraschino cherry, halves

½ cup butter

1 cup granulated sugar

2 eggs

1 teaspoon vanilla

2 cups all-purpose flour, sifted

2 teaspoons baking powder

½ teaspoon salt

½ cup milk

1 cup whipped cream (optional)

Directions

Preheat oven to 350°F. Spray skillet with non-stick cooking spray.

Melt the 2 tablespoons butter in large iron skillet (frying pan), on top of stove. Add brown sugar, mix well and turn off heat. Press brown sugar mixture evenly onto bottom of skillet.

Arrange peaches and cherries, in any pattern you prefer, on top of the brown sugar. Mix 1/2 cup softened butter and white sugar in bowl and blend well.

Add eggs, and blend. Next add the flour, baking powder, salt and milk and blend until creamy.

Add vanilla flavoring and blend. Spread batter on top of peaches and set pan on top of cookie sheet and bake for 1 hour.

Allow to cool for about 5 minutes, then run a knife along the edges of the skillet to loosen.

Place cake plate on top of skillet and invert, allowing cake to drop out of the skillet.

Serve warm with whipped cream on top.

Caramel Chocolate Chip Cookie Cake

Ingredients

1 (30 ounce) package refrigerated chocolate chip cookie dough

Caramel Layer

7 ounces caramel candies, soft

2 tablespoons heavy cream

Soft Cookie Dough Layer

8 ounces cream cheese, softened

4 tablespoons butter, softened

4 cups powdered sugar

1 tablespoon vanilla

$\frac{1}{2}$ cup semi-sweet chocolate chips, mini

Chocolate Glaze

$\frac{3}{4}$ cup semi-sweet chocolate chips

$\frac{1}{2}$ cup creamy peanut butter

4 tablespoons heavy cream

Directions

Preheat oven to 350ºF. Press cookie dough into the bottom of a 10-inch deep skillet. Bake for 18-22 minutes or until top layer is light golden brown and cookie has set in the center. Remove from oven, allow to cool for 20-30 minutes.

Prepare the caramel layer by melting caramel candies and heavy cream together in a medium pot, stirring constantly. Drizzle over cookie layer in the skillet. Place in fridge and allow to cool and set completely, for about 1 hour.

In a large bowl or stand mixer, beat cookie-dough ingredients together until smooth. Mixture should be thick, but spreadable. Spread on top of cooled caramel layer.

In a large microwave-safe bowl, microwave chocolate chips, peanut butter, and heavy cream together for 60 seconds. Whisk and return to microwave if needed. Microwave in 30 second bursts just until smooth. Spread glaze over cookie-dough layer. Place skillet in fridge and allow to cool completely before slicing and serving, about 30-45 minutes.

If the cookie has been stored in the fridge for longer than 1 hour, remove it from the fridge and let sit at room temperature for 30 minutes before slicing and serving.

Conclusion

With the right tricks, ingredients and recipes, you too can prepare delicious delicacies at your own home. All you need is the right source. This book helps you take the leap forward and brings you a little closer to your deepest wish to cook like a chef.

www.ingramcontent.com/pod-product-compliance
Lightning Source LLC
Chambersburg PA
CBHW071459070526
44578CB00001B/385